HEALING FROM TOXIC RELATIONSHIPS IN MARRIAGE, DATING AND INTERPERSONAL CONNECTIONS

BREAK FREE BY TAKING STEPS TOWARD RECOVERY AND REBUILDING SELF-ESTEEM, CONFIDENCE AND HEALTHY BOUNDARIES

ARIANE S. TURPIN

Copyright © 2024 Ariane S. Turpin

All rights reserved.

The content contained within this book may not be reproduced, duplicated or transmitted without direct written permission from the author or the publisher.

Under no circumstances will any blame or legal responsibility be held against the publisher, or author, for any damages, reparation, or monetary loss due to the information contained within this book. Either directly or indirectly. You are responsible for your own choices, actions, and results.

ISBN: 978-1-7389457-6-4 (Hardcover)

ISBN: 978-1-7389457-5-7 (Paperback)

ISBN: 978-1-7389457-4-0 (Ebook)

Legal Notice:

This book is copyright protected. This book is only for personal use. You cannot amend, distribute, sell, use, quote or paraphrase any part, or the content within this book, without the consent of the author or publisher.

Disclaimer Notice:

Please note the information contained within this document is for educational and entertainment purposes only. All effort has been executed to present accurate, up to date, and reliable, complete information. No warranties of any kind are declared or implied. Readers acknowledge that the author is not engaging in the rendering of legal, financial, medical or professional advice. The content within this book has been derived from various sources. Please consult a licensed professional before attempting any techniques outlined in this book.

*Some names and identifying details have been changed, and some events have been compressed.

By reading this document, the reader agrees that under no circumstances is the author responsible for any losses, direct or indirect, which are incurred as a result of the use of the information contained within this document, including, but not limited to, — errors, omissions, or inaccuracies.

Published by The Luxe North Publishing

Montreal, QC, Canada

www.arianeturpin.com

CONTENTS

Introduction ix

1. CHAPTER 1: RECOGNIZING THE SIGNS OF TOXIC RELATIONSHIPS — 1
   - 1.1 Understanding Toxic Relationships — 2
   - 1.2 A Look at the Statistics — 8
   - 1.3 Warning Bells - Identifying the Red Flags — 13
   - 1.4 The Hard Decision - Ending Toxic Relationships — 18

2. CHAPTER 2: UNDERSTANDING THE ROOT CAUSES OF TOXIC BEHAVIOR — 24
   - 2.1 The Shadows of Childhood — 25
   - 2.2 Mental Health – The Invisible Chains — 31
   - 2.3 Power Dynamics and the Cycle of Abuse — 35
   - 2.4 Intergenerational Echoes — 39
   - 2.5 From Understanding to Transformation — 44

3. CHAPTER 3: HEALING AND RECOVERY — 45
   - 3.1 Acknowledging and Processing Pain — 46
   - 3.2 Coping Mechanisms and Healing Tools — 50
   - 3.3 Therapy and Counseling as Sources of Support — 55
   - 3.4 Embracing Self-Care: Nurturing Your Self — 60

4. CHAPTER 4: REBUILDING SELF-ESTEEM AND CONFIDENCE — 65
   - 4.1 Rediscovering Self-worth — 67
   - 4.2 Identifying and Challenging Negative Self-talk — 71
   - 4.3 Practicing Self-compassion and Self-love — 74
   - 4.4 Building Healthy Habits and Routines — 76

5. CHAPTER 5: ESTABLISHING HEALTHY BOUNDARIES — 81
   5.1 The Power of "No" — 82
   5.2 Effective Communication for Healthy Boundaries — 83
   5.3 Laying the Foundations: How to Set Boundaries — 84
   5.4 Enforcing Boundaries — 85
   5.5 The Bigger Picture: Self-care and Boundaries — 86

6. CHAPTER 6: FORGIVENESS AND CLOSURE — 88
   6.1 Understanding the Essence of Forgiveness — 90
   6.2 The Misconceptions Surrounding Forgiveness — 91
   6.3 Journeying Towards Closure — 97
   6.4 The Release of Anger and Bitterness — 102
   6.5 Crafting a Life of Peace and Purpose — 107

7. CHAPTER 7: OVERCOMING CODEPENDENCY — 113
   7.1 Signs and Symptoms of Codependency — 114
   7.2 Root Causes of Codependency — 115
   7.3 Breaking the Chains: Building Self-Reliance — 117
   7.4 The Journey Ahead — 118

8. CHAPTER 8: MOVING FORWARD WITH HEALTHY RELATIONSHIPS — 120
   8.1 Healthy Relationship Essentials — 121
   8.2 Nurturing Relationship Bonds — 126
   8.3 Building a Deeper Connection — 131
   8.4 The Impact of Healthy Relationships — 136

Conclusion	139
About the Author	143
Also by Ariane S. Turpin	145
Resources	147
References	149

FREE GIFT #1 FOR MY READERS

Just for you! Get this free ebook as my gift to you for being my valued reader. You will have access to 5 weeks' worth of journal prompts (a total of 35) which serve as your invitation to explore different aspects of  your journey on the self-love path, encouraging deep self-reflection and nurturing a positive mindset.

Visit ebook.arianeturpin.com/selflovejournal or scan the above QR code.

INTRODUCTION

"Celebrate endings, for they precede new beginnings."

— JONATHAN LOCKWOOD HUIE

I remember very clearly standing outside my apartment and looking up at the stars on the vast horizon. I wondered how something that started out so beautifully could turn into the cage that held my spirit captive. One of many nights when the weight of a bad relationship made it hard for me to breathe was around my chest, thus why I had to step outside to catch some fresh air. It slowly choked out the joy, freedom, and light in my life, like a vine moving into my mind.

If you are reading this, you may have been in or are in a situation that is toxic and makes you feel trapped. It is a sad but disturbingly common story that people of all ages, genders, backgrounds, and socioeconomic levels can relate to.

But first, let's be clear: what is a bad relationship? In her groundbreaking book *Toxic People (1995)*, Dr. Lillian Glass defined it as any connection where there isn't enough support, there is a lot of conflict, and there is competition and disrespect. People in this relationship always feel belittled, unappreciated, and mentally drained. Someone like a partner, friend, neighbor, or even family member could do it.

Being in this kind of a relationship can be very painful. Being alone, having endless self-doubt, and feeling like you're walking on eggshells are all things that many people wish they could wake up from. It might have been a quick realization or some advice whispered to you by a worried friend that set you off on the path to recognizing your involvement in this web and getting help. No matter what brought you here, know that this is a brave and important step.

I want these pages to be your support on the rough path from being hurt to getting better. The goal of this book is to be your guide, showing you how to leave a bad relationship behind and find love and healthy relationships for yourself. I am sharing the knowledge that I have gained over many years, including lessons learned and personal stories.

I've been on the same rough road you are. I've been through the same sorrow and problems, and have come out on the other side stronger, smarter, and with pure, caring love. My goal is for you to also be able to get out and start over.

Imagine a life where you feel loved and supported every morning, where your feelings are safe and understood, and where love means growth. This is not a dream of a perfect world; it is a very real possibility. Let me assure you that there is a way to a better life.

You're not alone. Healing is not just a possibility—it's a promise.

Welcome to your new beginning.

CHAPTER 1: RECOGNIZING THE SIGNS OF TOXIC RELATIONSHIPS

Melissa* looked in the mirror and noticed the tired lines that were slowly showing up on her face. She used to be very young. The lively, bubbly woman she remembered seemed like a ghost from a past life, and the sad image staring back at her was like a faint echo. Piece by piece, her health was getting worse every day, but she held on to the dream that things would get better.

It hurt to think about the past because the bruise on her arm was still new and sore. It stood out against her pale skin like a sore thumb, an unsightly mark where there used to be smooth skin. Close by, the broken pieces of her once-loved vase were all over the floor. Each piece was a sharp memory of the violent encounter that had destroyed it. After being filled with fresh flowers, this vase, a gift from her mother, now lay broken, just like her spirit.

Still, it was this scene that finally woke her up. She had hardly noticed how her sense of self-worth was slowly slipping away, how her emotions were slowly dying. But now, the obvious physical signs made it hard to ignore what was going on.

Unfortunately, Melissa's story is not unique. More often than most people think, these kinds of stories happen behind closed doors. The threat of toxic relationships is always present, whether they are between sexual partners, familial, or close friendships. These relationships cast long, dark shadows over the lives of many people, slowly eroding their essence.

A year or so after my relationship ended with an ex-partner, is when I only realized that he was manipulative and toxic. He was sweet and he tended to love-bomb me, but in the darker times, he hurt me not only with words but also physically, albeit unintentionally. He had some anger issues, and unfortunately, I was the one on the receiving end. I was young and naive and barely knew anything about romantic relationships.

1.1 UNDERSTANDING TOXIC RELATIONSHIPS

Love and trust are building blocks of healthy relationships. They are like guiding lights that show the way to growth, understanding, and unwavering love for each other. They are what tie people together and help them get through the hard parts of life by sharing stories and being close to each other.

These ties, on the other hand, become weak when someone is in a bad relationship. The supportive setting, which used to include shared laughter, mutual respect, and a safe place to be vulnerable, starts to fade. Instead, it changes into a place where people are scared and worried. There is a constant apprehension that any action or word could set off fear, making the pleasure of being with someone less enjoyable. The freedom to express oneself also decreases.

When people are in these kinds of relationships, love, respect, and trust, which should hold them together, start to fall apart. People often find themselves navigating a rough sea of emotions, longing for the shores of real affection and mutual respect that seem farther away as an atmosphere of uncertainty and fear takes over.

Beyond the Occasional Tiff

There will be times when things do not go well in your relationships. When you and someone with different beliefs, habits, and backgrounds come together, it is only normal that there will sometimes be disagreements. These short-lived clashes can even be beneficial because they can lead to growth, understanding, and a stronger bond as you work through your differences.

But there is a huge difference between these everyday disagreements and the constant chaos that happens in harmful relationships. When this happens, your arguments do not just turn into short-lived storms; they turn into constant hurricanes that do a lot of damage. You might always feel tension, making every interaction feel like a skirmish in a neverending battle no matter how hard you try to communicate. Here, disagreements are not just isolated issues to resolve; they are symptomatic of bigger problems that have not been dealt with yet, which often leads to pointless arguments and endless disputes with no real answers.

It is very important for you to discern these differences. While every relationship has its challenges, it is vital to tell the difference between a short-term problem and a harmful pattern that will not go away. Knowing the difference can mean the distinction between traveling through rough water for a short time and being swept away by rough seas all the time. Ask yourself if this only happened once or twice, or whether this happens almost every day, every week, or every time something else happens that triggers it. Be honest with yourself.

The Many Faces of Abuse

As you go through relationships, it is important to keep in mind that abuse does not always show up in ways that are easy to see. There are types of abuse that hurt people deeply and quietly, but they are especially sneaky because they don't leave marks on the body. When there is no

CHAPTER 1: RECOGNIZING THE SIGNS OF TOXIC RELAT... | 5

obvious sign, there is often doubt, both in the victim and in those close to them. Being invisible can make the pain worse because victims have to deal with their experiences alone and may even start to doubt their feelings.

There is no doubt that physical hurt is traumatic and devastating. However, it is only one type of abuse out there. Some people do not realize the emotional, verbal, and psychological abuse that is lurking around them, destroying their sense of self-worth, confidence, and truth. Covert types of abuse can be just as bad for you as a physical blow, wearing down your spirit over time.

It is important to treat this subject with care and respect. For many, seeing or talking about abuse can be upsetting. If you have or are going through these kinds of problems, you should know that your feelings are normal and that you're not alone. When conversations get too much, it is always okay to ask for help or step back. Your health is very important.

- **Emotional Manipulation:** This could manifest as guilt-tripping, gaslighting, or playing the perpetual victim. Such tactics distort one's perception of reality, often making them doubt their feelings and memories.
- **Verbal Abuse:** Words can scar deeper than any knife. Consistent belittling, shouting, or name-calling can erode one's self-worth over time.
- **Control and Isolation:** A toxic partner might try to control who you meet, what you wear, or even

what you think. They might isolate you from friends and family, making you more dependent on them and furthering the cycle of control.

The Trap of Toxicity

If you are in a bad relationship, you know what it is like to feel trapped. A person who is going through toxicity often feels like they are looking out from behind thick, unmovable bars. The world outside may look bright and full of options. You cannot make these bars out of steel; they are made from lies, manipulation, and an endless mental tug-of-war. The constant gaslighting, in which your view of reality is systematically skewed, makes this feeling of being confined even stronger, making the cage seem even harder to escape.

A warped sense of loyalty often grows in this cage. Even though the relationship is bad, the victim may hold on to the hope that it will get better, that the good times will soon outweigh the bad, that "things will get better." This hopeful optimism is praiseworthy, but it can make you blind to the harm that keeps happening.

Pressures from outside the situation make things even more difficult. Dependence on money can make the thought of leaving scary, like stepping into a deep hole. Norms and standards in society also play a part. Being afraid of being judged, having a "failed" relationship, or having to face the world by yourself can be crippling.

CHAPTER 1: RECOGNIZING THE SIGNS OF TOXIC RELAT... | 7

Realizing that you feel trapped and confined is a sign of understanding, though. It is the first and most important step toward freedom; it means realizing that you deserve more than being trapped in a bad relationship.

THE WIDE SPECTRUM OF TOXICITY

It is not just sexual relationships where toxic relationships can grow. In fact, its sneaky reach can get into a lot of different kinds of bonds, from the closeness of family ties to the fun of friendships and even the formalities of business links. Think about the parent who, because of their own unfulfilled hopes, sets impossible standards for their child. Or the friend who seems to be there for you but is always quick to make fun of your successes with a quick comment. And when someone is a boss and constantly makes fun of others, the workplace can become a battleground for daily emotional battles. Even though these situations are different, they all have one thing in common: they are all examples of unhealthy relationships.

Finding harmful people in your relationships is not just a way to learn more about yourself; it is also important for your mental and emotional health. It is important to tell the difference between a relationship that regularly drains your spirit and the natural ups and downs of relationships. Because mutual respect, love, and a sense of understanding are at the heart of all real connections, whether they are family, friend, or work-related.

No matter what part they play in our lives, everyone should be a source of support and happiness. It is not ideal to stay in a relationship that is toxic. To put it simply, it is bad for you. The first step is to see and accept this fact. Even though it might be hard to change, the trip only strengthens the belief that everyone deserves a life free from the shadows of unhealthy relationships.

1.2 A LOOK AT THE STATISTICS

When talking about relationships, it is pleasant to think that most of them are based on love, respect, and understanding for each other. From this point of view, many people push harmful relationships to the edges of discussion, seeing them as outliers in the vast world of human connections. As humans, we naturally look for love, care, and approval, so it's almost natural for us to think that these things are mostly present in the relationships we have.

But as we dig deeper and look at real-world facts and personal stories, this reassuring front starts to fall apart. When you let raw data and stories go uncensored, you get a very different and, to be honest, unsettling picture. The frequency of toxic relationships, whether they are romantic, familial, or platonic, shows up not just as random events, but as clear, recurring patterns that require reflection and recognition.

The Reality of Romantic Entanglements

Romantic relationships, often portrayed in culture as havens of love and mutual respect, can, in reality, harbor deeply troubling dynamics. According to startling statistics from the National Coalition Against Domestic Violence (NCADV), you might be surprised to learn that a significant number of individuals face physical harm in their intimate relationships. Specifically, almost 1 in 3 women (35.6%) and 1 in 4 men (28.5%) have experienced rape, physical violence, and/or stalking from their partners. These figures aren't merely statistical; they represent countless personal narratives of distress, pain, and betrayal in spaces meant for trust and safety.

Yet, physical harm is just one part of the issue. Beneath the noticeable signs of abuse lie various hidden forms of maltreatment that you might not be immediately aware of. Emotional distress, manipulation, gaslighting, and other psychological tactics can be just as damaging but often stay unspoken. You might wonder why these forms of abuse remain hidden. Many reasons exist, from societal judgment, fear of reprisal, to the internal belief that unless abuse leaves a visible mark, it's not "real." But you have to remember: emotional abuse *is* abuse.

This stark contrast between visible injuries and unseen emotional wounds emphasizes the urgency for you to broaden your comprehension of what abuse truly entails. A haunting thought to consider: if such vast numbers face clear physical harm, how many more might silently endure the less visible, yet equally painful, forms of abuse?

Unfortunately, it takes a woman an average of 7 attempts to leave an abusive relationship permanently. For men, there is no statistic available, but that doesn't discount the fact that they can also be victims/survivors. There is no "typical victim", anyone can be an abuser, and there is no one theory that explains the "why".

Beyond Physical Harm

When you hear the term "abuse," your mind might instantly conjure images of physical harm, visible scars, and clear acts of violence. However, the landscape of toxic relationships is far more intricate and layered than just the overt signs of physical mistreatment. While physical violence is undeniably one of the most recognizable indicators of abuse, it isn't the sole manifestation. There are many other insidious forms of mistreatment that you might encounter.

Emotional and psychological abuse often operates covertly, causing harm that may not be immediately evident but runs profoundly. Acts of manipulation, gaslighting, and persistent degradation might not manifest as tangible scars, yet they inflict lasting emotional and mental trauma that can persist for years or even a lifetime. Similarly, financial control, where one person exerts undue influence over another's finances, can induce feelings of helplessness and dependency. Although such forms of abuse might not result in immediate physical injury, they can erode your self-esteem, amplify feelings of powerlessness, and cultivate a pervasive sense of fear and distrust.

The subtlety of non-physical abuse can sometimes make you oblivious to its occurrence. The societal emphasis on visible signs of distress may lead you to discount or invalidate your experiences. However, recognizing and understanding these varied manifestations of abuse is important, especially if you find yourself entangled in such a relationship. It is a vital step toward seeking help, initiating healing, and eventually reclaiming your autonomy.

Familial Dynamics - The Silent Crisis

When we think about unhealthy relationships, the usual thought is about romantic ties. Under the surface, though, and often hidden by social norms and quiet, are the complicated and deeply rooted problems that make families toxic. A worrisome fact from a Forbes article in 2019 shows statistics that between 70% and 80% of Americans think their family relationships aren't working well, or in other words, dysfunctional. The fact that these numbers are so shocking shows how many problems people have in the relationships they are born into.

Family relationships can be complicated in many ways, such as when parents who have not dealt with their own problems put too much pressure on their children or when siblings fight and are angry with each other. There is also the generational circle of toxic behavior, in which abuse and dysfunctional behavior are passed down through the lineage, often without the person being aware of it. The basis of these patterns makes them very hard to deal with. Families do not choose to be together; they are born that way. These ties are strong because they are based on shared history, bloodlines, and often cultural and social standards. They can be hard to break, even when they are tense.

Still, the strength and longevity of these bonds make it even more important to address the hidden crisis that exists within them right away. For many, family is the main place where they find identity, support, and understanding. There is an urgent need for notice, intervention, and healing if this foundation is weak because it can affect every other part of a person's life.

FRIENDSHIPS AND FRENEMIES

A joint survey conducted by TODAY.com and SELF magazine in 2011 revealed that toxic friendships are a common experience, with 84% of women and 75% of men admitting they have had a toxic friend at some point. These toxic friends are often self-absorbed, overly critical, or unreliable, making relationships with them draining and difficult. Despite this, many people continue these friendships longer than is healthy due to guilt, familiarity, or the fear of losing the connection.

The survey also highlighted gender differences in toxic friendships, with women more likely to have toxic female friends and men more likely to have toxic male friends. Women's friendships often involve more emotional intimacy, leaving them more vulnerable to toxic behavior, while men's friendships are more activity-based, making them less prone to such issues. 83% of survey takers confessed that they had kept their friendship longer than was healthy because it was hard to break up with a friend, which is usually due to familiarity or something they find compelling with the person.

With these findings, it is important to reassess friendships regularly to ensure they are healthy and beneficial. While toxic friendships can be damaging, ending them often leads to relief and the opportunity to form healthier relationships. Some people, however, choose to "downgrade" toxic friends rather than cut them off entirely, finding ways to focus on the positive aspects of the relationship.

Statistics are more than just numbers; they can give you new ideas, make you think, and even start a change—which is precisely what our aim here is—to change and heal from toxic relationships. Toxic relationships affect a lot of people, which shows how important it is to raise awareness, educate people, and offer support. Every person needs relationships that make them feel better, not ones that bring them down. The numbers remind us of the journey we need to take together to make sure that bad relationships become the exceptions they should be.

1.3 WARNING BELLS - IDENTIFYING THE RED FLAGS

Each relationship is different, just like the people in it. Each has its own complexities and patterns. Still, some habits really stand out as clear signs of deeper, more serious problems.

Recognizing early signs of toxic dynamics in your relationships is like being able to spot storm clouds gathering in the distance, indicating potential trouble ahead. The sooner you identify these looming disturbances in your interactions, the better equipped you will be to safeguard your emotional and mental well-being.

Identifying these warning signs is not merely about preventing distress. It is about empowering yourself to actively shape the trajectory of your own experiences. By addressing these concerns as they emerge, you grant yourself the opportunity to redirect the relationship toward a more positive outcome. Timely intervention can facilitate constructive discussions, fostering understanding and collective growth.

However, this early detection can sometimes serve another purpose. It provides the clarity you might need to discern when a relationship is beyond repair. If you notice consistent patterns of toxicity, even in the initial phases, these can act as stark indicators suggesting it might be prudent for you to seek more supportive and harmonious environments.

The Many Guises of Toxicity

Every relationship has its unique dynamics, and certain patterns consistently emerge in toxic situations. While some signs are more obvious than others, the following

CHAPTER 1: RECOGNIZING THE SIGNS OF TOXIC RELA... | 15

list also includes subtler indicators that you should be aware of:

1. Emotional gaslighting
2. Persistent feelings of dread
3. Consistent belittlement
4. Isolation from loved ones
5. Financial control
6. Constantly shifting goalposts

Let's talk more about each one.

First point: Emotional gaslighting involves manipulating someone into doubting their own feelings, memories, or events. It can be as subtle as dismissing one's feelings or as overt as denying events that clearly took place. It could be in the form of small comments, hidden gestures, or even passive-aggressive behavior that can slowly destroy the mutual respect that is necessary for a healthy relationship.

Second point: If the thought of interacting with a person or entering a particular environment consistently induces anxiety, it is a significant red flag. Communication that turns into constant aggression is just as scary. If you cannot have calm, helpful conversations and cannot voice your concerns or deal with problems without anger seeping in, the relationship can quickly become toxic. Relationships should predominantly evoke feelings of safety and comfort, not persistent dread.

Third point: This is not about the occasional jest or lighthearted banter. Constantly diminishing someone's achievements, aspirations, or feelings, especially in public or in front of peers, is a clear warning sign. Getting disrespected over and over is never a good thing.

Fourth point: If someone constantly tries to cut you off from friends, family, or support networks, it is often a tactic to increase dependence on them. Your social interactions are being limited, and the partner may decide who you can hang out with. At the same time, they may use fear, duty, or guilt as an emotional tool.

Fifth point: Restricting access to shared financial resources or controlling how one spends their personal finances can be indicative of deeper control issues.

Sixth point: A situation where no achievement is ever good enough, and the standards of approval keep changing can be incredibly destabilizing.

Recognizing Patterns Across Different Relationships

While this chapter has painted broad strokes, it is crucial to realize that toxic patterns can manifest in various types of relationships.

For example in business relationships, a business partner or colleague persistently undermines efforts, takes undue credit, or creates hostile environments. In romantic partnerships, beyond the obvious signs, other red flags include invasion of personal space, incessant jealousy, and

CHAPTER 1: RECOGNIZING THE SIGNS OF TOXIC RELA... | 17

refusing to respect boundaries. In familial relationships, family members can sometimes use the depth of their bond to manipulate emotions. Watch out for guilt-tripping, emotional blackmail, or consistently crossing established boundaries.

Understanding the warning signs in a relationship is like having a flashlight to navigate the complexities of human interactions. This clarity is invaluable as it helps navigate through the murkiness that can arise from doubts or misunderstandings. Recognizing these signs not only provides clarity but also empowers you to make informed decisions rooted in self-awareness and self-worth. It can open doors to beneficial outcomes, such as seeking counseling, reinforcing personal boundaries, or, when deemed necessary, taking the difficult step of creating distance.

Yet, it is crucial to approach this understanding with nuance and sensitivity. Every indication does not necessarily spell doom for the relationship. Relationships, in their essence, are intricate weaves of emotions, experiences, and memories. A single issue does not always mean the entire bond is flawed. Viewing potential red flags should be more about contemplation and communication rather than immediate judgment. For some, these signs could stir up past traumas or sensitivities, underscoring the importance of handling them with care and ensuring discussions take place in a supportive environment.

Being vigilant about potential toxicity is essential, but it is equally important to temper this awareness with compassion—for both yourself and the other party involved. The ultimate aim is not to cast blame or label but to foster relationships where every participant feels acknowledged, valued, and cherished.

1.4 THE HARD DECISION - ENDING TOXIC RELATIONSHIPS

Realizing you are in a bad relationship can be like waking up with an unexpected weight pulling hard on your heart and soul. This burden can make a person feel a lot of different feelings, like shock, anger, deep sadness, and sometimes a gnawing guilt. Each feeling can feel like a flood, and for many, getting through this storm is a painful and confusing journey.

It gets more complicated for people whose relationships have been going on for a long time or are very close. When people share memories, moments, and important moments, they can blur the lines between what is harmful and what is not. Not only do you have to deal with your current feelings, you also have to make peace with a past that seems to be seen through a different lens now. This recalibration can bring up painful memories from the past, making some people have strong emotions. Not only does the process help these people recognize what happened, but it also helps them heal from hurts that keep coming back.

There is, however, a glimmer of hope in all of this mental chaos: the act of recognizing. Recognizing these thoughts, no matter how scary they are, shows how strong and resilient you are. It is a brave first step toward not only knowing what is going on but also getting back your peace, independence, and sense of self-worth.

One example is Bella*, a full-time student who had been with her boyfriend for several years. She and her boyfriend lived together, split their bills together, and even have a dog who loves them both so much. She had come to the realization one day that she was in a toxic relationship with her boyfriend and wanted to get out of it. She did not know how she could manage being a full-time student while working to pay bills and at the same time take care of herself and her dog, who is also her emotional support dog, because of her anxiety. She opened up to her girl community for advice, and that was the great first step that she took.

Like Bella, it is important to remember to be kind to yourself as you go through this process. Know that it is okay to ask for help, lean on people who can support you, and put your health first. You are not the only one going through this, and every kind of step you take toward understanding brings you closer to a place of healing and strength.

The Emotional Struggle of Letting Go

Often, the scary thought of ending the relationship quickly overshadows the sudden clarity that comes with realizing you're in an unhealthy one. When you add this understanding to an array of memories, feelings, and fears, the thought of untangling becomes an emotional journey. In a strange way, letting go is one of the most soul-stirring things you can ever think about, even though it goes against your natural desire to protect yourself.

In the middle of this emotional landscape are memories of laughs, private times, and important events that once showed how close they were. These memories can sometimes make the present seem more positive, blurring the harsh facts and making it hard to tell the difference. Outside forces make this already complicated tapestry even more difficult to understand. Social expectations, the weight of family views, or even shared responsibilities can keep someone from making a decision, making them even less likely to take that first step.

There is also a strong compass: a deep knowledge of your own worth and well-being. Realizing that these are essential and cannot be changed can help you see things more clearly, even when things are very confusing. With this new point of view, the choice to step away changes in its core. It changes from something that feels like abandonment or betrayal to a deep act of self-love and self-respect —a strong statement that you deserve a place that cares for, values, and respects your very being.

Navigating the Exit Safely

In order to get out of a toxic relationship, you have to do more than just deal with your feelings and thoughts. You also have to take realistic steps that will protect your safety and well-being. This journey is like finding your way through a maze; every turn leads to something new, but you have to be very careful and know what you are doing ahead of time.

At the very beginning of this maze is a shield of safety that will not bend. Safety, both emotionally and physically, is very important. In the same way that you might wear safety gear when going out in a storm, having a strong support system around you protects you from possible harm. Friends, family, and professionals can not only help you feel better emotionally, but they can also give you useful tips and plans. Their combined knowledge and help can be very helpful, giving focus, strength, and sometimes even safety.

It takes even more careful planning to get out of a relationship where abuse is a sign of its toxic nature. Letting trusted people know about the choice to leave makes sure that others are aware and can help if needed. It can be very important to plan confrontations in public places or make sure that no one is alone during them if they have to happen. It can also be very helpful to talk to a lawyer when things are happening that could be illegal or when someone is violating your rights. This means that while the heart wants freedom, the mind has to plan the best way to get there.

Resources and Support

It can feel like navigating a thick, overwhelming forest when you are trying to understand and get away from toxic relationships. But it is important to know that this forest is not impossible to get through—there are established paths and guides ready to help. There are a lot of organizations, helplines, and neighborhood groups that are devoted to helping people who are caught up in toxic relationships. There is a wide range of services available, from helping people in an instant crisis to providing counseling and therapy services that aim to heal emotional wounds and strengthen the spirit.

Here are a few of these resources:

- **National Domestic Violence Hotline (US)** - Visit the website at thehotline.org or call 1-800-799-SAFE (7233). The hotline provides service referrals to agencies across the US including Puerto Rico, Guam, and the US Virgin Islands
- **One Love** - Visit the website at joinonelove.org
- **Assaulted Women's Helpline (Canada)** - Visit the website at https://www.awhl.org/ or call 1-866-863-0511
- **National Domestic Abuse Helpline (UK)** - Visit the website at https://www.nationaldahelpline.org.uk/ or call 0808 2000 247
- **National Domestic Family and Sexual Violence Counselling Service (Australia)** - Visit the website at https://www.1800respect.org.au/ or call 1-800-RESPECT (737-732)

If you are in immediate danger, however, it is best to call

your local emergency number - 911 (US/Canada), 999 (UK), or 000 or 112 (Australia).

Going through these resources not only gives you useful tools, but it also helps you remember that you are not fighting this battle alone. It is comforting to know that there are skilled experts and caring communities who are aware of the complexities of your situation and are ready to offer their support. This support network can be the lifesaver that pulls you out of the murkiness of toxicity, whether in certain times of trouble or as part of your journey to recovery.

There is no doubt that bad, unhealthy relationships can leave long-lasting and often crippling marks on anyone's mind. So, whenever you take the step toward understanding, recognizing, and taking action, hope shines through the darkness. Without a doubt, this journey is hard, but it is also a trip of great courage, strength, and self-discovery. With the right tools and the help of invaluable support, you can leave the confines of toxic dynamics and enter the refreshing and freeing world of healthy, caring, and fulfilling relationships. Keep going, you've got this!

CHAPTER 2: UNDERSTANDING THE ROOT CAUSES OF TOXIC BEHAVIOR

*A*s Melissa looked at what she saw, the angry words were still reverberating in the room. Broken pieces of glass were all over the floor. Each piece represented a relationship that used to offer love and understanding but was now in pieces. It was hard to breathe because of how tense the air was. It was very different from when they were laughing together, which filled the room. As she watched the agitated figure walking in front of her, she could not help but wonder: What deep-seated pain or trauma had driven this person to act in such a destructive way?

Melissa felt anger and irritation, which were normal responses, but she also felt compassion. They had a history of deep-seated sadness and unaddressed emotional wounds that often led to such unstable behavior. Maybe the anger that was showing now was just a mask that covered up deeper wounds and weaknesses from a hard past.

As we go through this chapter, I encourage you to do so with both empathy and understanding. We want to bring attention to the unseen and often ignored triggers that lead to harmful behavior by trying to unravel and understand their complex layers. This will help allow yourself the feeling of compassion while also highlighting the urgent need for your healing and self-awareness.

2.1 THE SHADOWS OF CHILDHOOD

From sharing laughter with your parents as a child to facing challenges during your teenage years, your childhood is a compilation of events, emotions, and lessons that mold your adulthood. These early experiences, absorbed during your most impressionable years, often lay the groundwork for the roles you embrace as an adult. Many of the roles you now inhabit—be it the affectionate partner, the fierce guardian, or the resilient individual—stem from the narratives you internalized in your youth.

Much like how the setting sun casts elongated shadows, distorting and amplifying even the tiniest objects, the incidents from your formative childhood years can greatly influence your behaviors and decisions in adulthood. Each word of praise, critique, joyous occasion, and distressing event you encountered during those important pivotal years can resonate throughout the subsequent stages of your life in the decades that follow.

Because a child's mind is soft and open, it takes in everything around it like a sponge. These gathered feelings you had in your childhood— whether they are of affection, neglect, comfort, or trouble—seep deep into the mind. Even if you cannot always see it on the surface, their depth and impact often go deeper than you think, shaping your actions, beliefs, and reactions in your adult life.

Trauma, Neglect, and Abuse - The Unseen Scars

Childhood trauma is not uncommon, with 2 out of 3 children experiencing this in some form, according to the Substance Abuse and Mental Health Services Administration (SAMHSA) (*Lebow, 2021*). Keep in mind that what you may find traumatic may not be the same for someone else. We all experience life in different ways, but the trauma, neglect, or abuse are all recognized to have long-lasting effects. These experiences aren't mere memories tucked away in the recesses of your mind; they actively shape your interactions and perceptions in the present and will continue to do so in the future. Recognizing this truth is necessary, but it might evoke intense emotions, so it is important to be kind and understanding when talking about it.

For you, if you have experienced mental turmoil, physical harm, or the isolating void of neglect during your childhood, it is not just about recalling past incidents. Those memories are very much alive. They might resurface unpredictably—sometimes as fragmented, elusive shadows at the periphery of your consciousness, and at

CHAPTER 2: UNDERSTANDING THE ROOT CAUSES OF ... | 27

other times as vivid, intense flashbacks that make the present seem less real for a moment. Realizing how strong these memories are does not mean relieving pain; it means comprehending its scope and impact.

If you think that merely letting time pass alone will erase the effects of such deep events, then you have to understand that you are mistaken as this is often not the case. These memories do not usually fade away; instead, they tend to become deeply ingrained, subtly influencing your decisions, actions, and emotions. However, with compassion, self-awareness, and a commitment to healing, you can navigate these memories. When you draw from your innate resilience, there is a path to recovery and a deeper understanding of yourself.

EMOTIONAL WOUNDS AND THEIR OUTWARD MANIFESTATIONS

All wounds, if you neglect them, have the potential to intensify, and emotional wounds are no exception. Just as a physical wound left unattended might become infected and more painful, any emotional traumas from your childhood that remain unresolved can grow in complexity and impact you deeply as an adult. These emotional scars can have far-reaching implications, often extending beyond what you might immediately recognize or feel.

You might notice that at times, you display certain behaviors or reactions. Maybe you've experienced sudden outbursts of anger, periods of emotional instability, or found yourself frequently desiring solitude and isolating yourself. These are merely external signs of an underlying turmoil, a storm of pain, lingering questions, and unresolved emotions. This internal conflict isn't just about living in the past; it's an ongoing dialogue between past traumas and current coping mechanisms.

Consider, for instance, if as a child you always yearned for someone to listen to you, but constantly felt overlooked or ignored. Now, as an adult, you might find yourself raising your voice, not because you're naturally combative, but because there's a deep-rooted need to be finally acknowledged. Or, if you faced consistent neglect during your formative years, you might, as an adult, find yourself constantly seeking validation. Alternatively, you might shy away from forming deep relationships, fearing further rejection or neglect, choosing instead to protect yourself with walls that are hard to break down.

Even though these reactions stem from past experiences, they also symbolize your yearning for understanding, empathy, and healing. Recognizing the connection between your past and your present is the first step toward bridging that gap.

The Journey of Recognition and Healing

As the first hint of dawn appears, awareness appears, signifying optimism and fresh starts. Comprehending the complex interplay between your early experiences and how they materialize in your adult life is essential to establishing the foundation for recovery. Even while this path is extremely personal, it frequently benefits from outside guidance, whether it comes from counseling, therapy, or the steady presence of dependable connections.

Looking far into your history is an investigation of understanding rather than a simple memory test. It's about creating a tapestry of empathy, not about blaming situations, caregivers, or even yourself. It's about seeing prior joys and sorrows as essential chapters that have molded your life story rather than as discrete occurrences. It can be emotionally draining to acknowledge this, but it's important to keep in mind that this process is about purging, healing, and eventually transcending old wounds rather than reopening them.

There are a multitude of ways to start this life-changing adventure. In therapeutic environments, where qualified specialists offer frameworks and tools to process and heal, some people find comfort and clarity. Others may find solace in support groups, where the basis for group healing is the sharing of personal experiences. And for others, time itself, in conjunction with reflection and self-awareness, has a healing quality all its own.

Your journey is one of empowerment, no matter which road you choose. It's about taking back control of your story, letting go of ominous shadows, and accepting a future in which your past is recognized, comprehended, and integrated—rather than being a source of limitation for you.

Emerging from the Shadows

The formative years of childhood are filled with a complicated tapestry of experiences, lessons learned, pleasures, and horrors. It leaves profound traces that direct our activities, shape our perspectives, and impact how we connect with others as we grow into adulthood. Even so, these formative experiences don't leave a permanent mark on you or determine how your life will unfold. Although it may have shaped you, your past does not limit you.

Understanding the shadows left by previous traumas and wounds is the first signpost leading to recovery. It's an admission that although some experiences and events have had an impact on you, they don't have to determine who you are now or will be in the future. It is possible to face these shadows with the correct help, whether through counseling, caring relationships, or inner strength. You need to have understanding, acceptance, and openness to transformation on your part, rather than a conflict of resistance.

As you set out on this path of self-examination and recovery, you will discover that stepping out of the shadows involves more than just moving on from the past. It's about bringing understanding to it, drawing lessons from suffering, and encouraging development in the face of difficulty. It's about giving your stories a new meaning and contour so that they speak to you with courage, optimism, and a revitalized sense of purpose.

You—and every person—deserve the opportunity to enter a better present and future, regardless of your history—a future characterized by self-awareness, sincere relationships, and the limitless possibilities that present themselves when you break free from the bonds of the past and welcome the brightness of fresh starts.

2.2 MENTAL HEALTH – THE INVISIBLE CHAINS

Your mind is like the command center for all your relationships; it shapes how you respond, connect, and bond with others. Your thoughts, emotions, and instincts significantly influence the interactions you have every day. And while mental health might seem like a topic for therapy sessions or medical discussions, it is deeply intertwined with your daily life, impacting and molding the way you relate to those around you.

Your mental state, influenced by your past experiences, beliefs, and emotions, guides how you see and interact with the world. But it is not set in stone. Various factors can shift and sometimes disrupt this state, and mental health conditions are major players in this. Think of them like unexpected storms that can alter your mental landscape. Conditions like anxiety or depression can overshadow your thoughts, significantly altering your behaviors, actions, and how you perceive situations.

Imagine you are an actor in life's grand play. While many actors get to choose their roles, when dealing with a mental health condition, it might feel like someone else has rewritten your script. Where your lines once spoke of joy and enthusiasm, depression might replace them with hopelessness and despair. The script of anxiety might introduce lines filled with constant worry and overthinking. These altered scripts play out in real-life, influencing how you engage in the story of your relationships.

Recognizing the connection between your relationships and mental health is vital. By understanding how mental health conditions can change your outlook, you can foster greater patience, empathy, and forge deeper connections, especially when engaging with those navigating these challenges.

The Dual Nature of Mental Disorders

From the research I gathered from the Discovery Mood & Anxiety Program and the National Center for Biotechnology Information (NCBI), it becomes clear how deeply mental health challenges can influence behavior. Consider what it might feel like to be in the shoes of people with an anxiety disorder, for example. It's like walking on a tightrope. You are constantly on edge, perpetually on high alert, your senses keenly aware of even the smallest changes in your surroundings. This continuous alertness acts like an internal alarm that never turns off, making you perceive even harmless situations as threats or interpret neutral signals as aggressive or hostile.

Imagine living with this level of stress daily. Like a kettle boiling and ready to whistle, this tension might sometimes erupt. Small incidents could provoke major reactions. To others, your responses might seem over the top, but given the heightened state you're in, they feel entirely appropriate to you.

Conversely, if you are battling depression, your world might often seem shrouded in twilight. It is not just about feeling down; it is like a dense fog that changes how you see everything, draining your joy and energy. This haze can make even close relationships feel like a maze. You might find yourself pulling away, not because you don't care, but because you're trying to shield yourself from the overwhelming tide of emotions.

Recognizing how these conditions affect your actions and reactions is important. By understanding them, you can create a space of empathy for yourself, making sense of behaviors that might otherwise seem puzzling. It's a crucial step towards healing and meaningful connections.

BEYOND THE STEREOTYPES

Making the distinction between intentional behavior and unconscious reactions is crucial. The responses displayed by people who are struggling with mental illnesses are not impulsive decisions or resistance. As an alternative, they result from complex imbalances and disruptions in the complex chemistry and circuitry of the brain. These expressions are often the brain's coping mechanism with internal turmoil, rather than deliberate or conscious choices.

However, cultural perspectives, frequently tainted with misunderstandings and biases, have a tendency to oversimplify and categorize these intricate actions. Someone suffering from anxiety may be hurriedly called "overly sensitive" or "dramatic," whereas someone struggling with depression may be written off as "unmotivated," "apathetic," or even "antisocial." But these designations hardly begin to capture the complex physiological and psychological undercurrents at work. They reduce these people's issues to mere phrases, diminishing their genuine experiences.

Therefore, it is critical to dispel and get beyond these condescending prejudices. The first stages in creating a more accepting, compassionate, and knowledgeable culture are going deeper, trying to comprehend things more deeply, and showing unwavering compassion. Fostering a society where mental health is respected and approached delicately is our collective responsibility.

Navigating Relationships with Awareness

Mental health and interpersonal relationships are closely connected. Your mental state impacts every interaction you have, from happy moments to disagreements. By recognizing this connection, you can form strong, deep, and meaningful relationships.

When you genuinely realize how much mental health matters, your viewpoint completely changes. You start to go past the obvious responses and instead focus on the complex network of events, feelings, and illnesses that could be affecting the other person's behavior. This realization creates the conditions for empathy to grow, enabling you to swap out hasty conclusions for sincere comprehension. Unexpectedly, your acquaintance who often cancels plans might not be "flaky" after all; instead, they might be suffering from social anxiety. It is possible that a coworker who frequently comes across as aloof is quietly fighting depression.

Recognizing how their illness affects their relationships and getting help can have a profoundly positive effect on someone who is struggling with mental health issues. Professional therapies can help empower them to manage symptoms and promote healthier, more meaningful interactions. These interventions might take the form of counseling, medicine, or holistic treatments. A healthy balance between mental health and fulfilling relationships may be difficult to achieve, but it is attainable with the correct resources and assistance, as long as they are willing and committed to take forward steps for the better.

2.3 POWER DYNAMICS AND THE CYCLE OF ABUSE

In your interactions with others, you might notice that power dynamics often come into play. These dynamics give a clear picture of how influence is distributed and exercised in your relationships. Picture it like this: Just as a puppeteer controls a puppet's movements with strings, these power dynamics subtly dictate the balance of control in many of your interpersonal exchanges.

These dynamics might show up in small, barely noticeable behaviors. Maybe it's in a gentle suggestion someone makes to you or a seemingly innocent gesture that, upon reflection, carries a hint of control. At other times, these dynamics can be blatant, where someone clearly exerts dominance over you. Whether you realize it or not, there might be instances where you find yourself either in a dominating role or in a submissive one, shaping the pace and direction of the relationship.

It is essential for you to understand that these dynamics don't always arise from ill intentions. They might come from cultural backgrounds, past experiences, or inherent personality traits. Regardless of their origin, it's important for you to recognize and address them, especially if they start bordering on manipulation. By doing so, you can ensure that your relationships remain balanced, respectful, and mutually beneficial.

The Cycle of Abuse: An Incessant Loop

The complexities of toxic relationships frequently take the form of patterns, loops that trap the parties involved in an unending round of highs and lows. The "cycle of abuse," also referred to as the "cycle of violence," a phrase that properly describes the recurring nature of these relationships, is among the most uncomfortable of these patterns. This cycle goes through four stages, from enticing the players into an unceasing loop of building tension, which results in an incident of abuse such as explosive confrontation, to fleeting moments of reconciliation, and finally a false lull of peace (*Walker, 1979, as cited in Healthline, 2020*).

This false calm is especially dangerous because it gives people a false sense of security by leading them to assume that the storm has gone and brighter times are ahead. But the roots of the next war are already there, waiting to burst through this apparent quiet. Gradually, the tension rises once more, reaching yet another breaking point before the dance of reconciliation ensues. This relationship's recurring nature not only keeps things going, but it also fosters a climate of uncertainty where people are always on guard, waiting for the next storm.

Because the abuse is recurrent, it is difficult for victims to identify it, much less escape its grip. This very pattern is what often keeps them bound together in the hopes that the peaceful times would one day become the norm in their relationship. The first step to escaping its bonds and pursuing more positive relationship dynamics is realizing this cycle.

To explain further, these are the four parts to the cycle:

1. **Tension building:** During this phase, the air is thick with impending conflict. Minor disagreements might escalate, communication diminishes, and the victim often feels the need to appease the abuser, walking on proverbial eggshells to avoid igniting an explosive situation.

2. **Incident of abuse or violence:** This is the phase where the abuse becomes overt and undeniable. It can range from verbal lashings and emotional manipulations to physical violence.
3. **Reconciliation:** Often termed the "honeymoon phase," this period is marked by apologies, promises of change, and sometimes, grand romantic gestures. The abuser may express profound remorse, and the victim, often clinging to the hope of genuine change, may forgive and try to move forward.
4. **Calm:** This period is characterized by a relative peace, wherein the relationship seems to revert to a healthier pattern. However, it's often a deceptive lull, as underlying issues remain unresolved, setting the stage for the cycle to recommence.

Unraveling the Power Struggles

No matter if you are rich or poor, what nationality or ethnic background you have, or what your civil status is, you can be affected by abuse or violence resulting from power dynamics that frequently serve as the foundation for unhealthy relationships. At the core of it is an intense urge for dominance. Keep in mind that "a survivor of domestic abuse does not need to experience physical abuse to be abused" (*Peace Over Violence, 2023*). This is not just about wanting control for control's sake. This need often stems from deep-rooted insecurities, learned behaviors from earlier life experiences, or past traumas. Instead of addressing these vulnerabilities, the dominant party might choose to exert control over their partner, compromising their emotional and physical well-being.

Now, for those on the receiving end of this toxic dynamic, it can feel like navigating a storm of conflicting emotions and external pressures. You might feel trapped, with a swirling mix of fear, genuine affection, financial concerns, and sometimes societal expectations influencing your decisions. This mix can create a distorted lens, causing you to waver between wanting to safeguard yourself and hoping for a change. Love and affection, the need for financial security, or the desire for societal acceptance can become heavy weights, making the journey towards self-liberation an incredibly challenging one.

2.4 INTERGENERATIONAL ECHOES

You are a unique tapestry, an intricate work of art woven from a mix of inherited traits, life experiences, and genetic predispositions. Your beliefs, values, and tendencies don't just arise from spontaneous reactions to the world. Who you are is influenced by countless voices and experiences that have echoed through time from past generations. When you interact with others, you are not just acting in the present moment; you are channeling a legacy and conveying your origin.

In your relationships and interactions, it is important to recognize the truth behind the adage: history often repeats itself, especially when it is not understood or acknowledged. Have you ever wondered why certain reactions or behaviors, especially those that puzzle or distress you, seem familiar or repetitive? Often, these can be traced back to patterns you've learned from your parents or guardians, who in turn also may have learned from their own parents or guardians.

Acknowledging these patterns and understanding their origins can be transformative. When you recognize that some of your challenges might not just be individual quirks but parts of a more extensive, multi-generational narrative, it encourages introspection, but you need to be careful not to make it an excuse to allow the negative behaviors to continue.

THE RIPPLE EFFECT OF CHILDHOOD MALTREATMENT

Childhood adversity affects people for a long time. As children are naturally impressionable, they are a lot like clay—they take on the shape of the hands that shape them and the surroundings they are in. Every action, word, and encounter leaves a mark that shapes their growth in a subtle way. Abuse, neglect, or mistreatment of these young people leave deep marks that usually stay with them as adults. Studies do indicate, however, that it is a combination of environmental, familial, and individual factors that either increase or decrease the risk of abuse and its effects from one generation to the next (*Greene et al., 2020*).

When you are young, these kinds of events do not just fade away into your memories. They change into ideas, attitudes, and patterns of behavior that shape how a person interacts with the world, whether they are aware of it or not. For example, a child who grew up in a home where fights happened often might have a skewed view of love and relationships, going back and forth between seeing aggressive behavior as normal and being filled with fear and dread.

When a kid is constantly made fun of or put down, they may carry those feelings into adulthood and struggle with deep-seated insecurities and low self-worth. There are two different ways that these inner battles could show up in the outside world: they could keep the cycle going by projecting these behaviors onto others, or they could always be looking for approval, trying to fill the void that began in their childhood.

The long-lasting effects of child abuse show how important early intervention is and how important nurturing, positive settings are in shaping the futures of young minds. As a society, we work to break the chains of intergenerational trauma, and finding out where these trends come from is important for everyone.

Breaking the Chain: The Challenge and the Hope

The idea of intergenerational toxicity is woeful. Noting that these patterns are highly ingrained, it is important to stress that they are not unbreakable chains that hold someone back. A simple but powerful act of acceptance can often be the start of the path to healing and change. People can start to change when they stop, think, and figure out that some of their actions are not really who they are but are instead echoes of past trauma.

Seeking help from a professional becomes a sign of hope on this path of change. Professionals, such as therapists and counselors trained to deal with such complicated emotional issues, can help people make sense of these passed-down traumas. It is not enough to just look into the past for therapeutic reasons; it is also important to understand what it means, deal with the pain, and plan a future that does not follow the inherited road of toxicity. Clearly, the goal is to avoid passing on the heavy burden of past tragedies to the next generation.

Also, having shared events and being strong as a group has its own power. Intergenerational trauma support groups, forums, and organizations offer comfort and a sense of community. People can find not only sympathetic ears here, but also a source of strength and strategies among the shared stories and intertwined paths. They are paving the way for healing by thinking about things together and helping each other. This shows that even though the wounds of the past may be deep, there is endless room for renewal and growth.

The Promise of a New Legacy

Your family tree is more than just a list of names and faces; it is the weight of experiences, feelings, and habits. Acknowledging these echoes can set off a chain reaction for many, evoking memories and feelings that are deeply ingrained but frequently tinged with conflict and suffering. Approaching this information with the utmost compassion is imperative, as many people carry the weight of previous generations with immense inner pain and frequently in silence.

But there is a ray of optimism amid these ominous echoes. Even though their experience has shaped them, each person is the author of their own story. Each one has the chance to write a story that differs from the upsetting narratives of the past with reflection, resiliency, and the appropriate assistance. Releasing oneself from these generational cycles is a healing process rather than a rebellion. It is about taking back control of one's own destiny and realizing that, although history matters, the present and the future are canvases just ready to be filled with bright, new paint.

Although leaving a legacy can carry a heavy weight, every day holds the possibility of breaking patterns and creating new legacies. It is a promise that things can be different tomorrow if you work for it and are conscious of it. We can make sure that the lasting effects we leave behind for future generations are ones of hope, healing, and harmonious relationships rather than ones of sorrow and toxicity by deliberately choosing love, understanding, and respect.

2.5 FROM UNDERSTANDING TO TRANSFORMATION

Past traumas, untreated emotional scars, and patterns learned during our formative years frequently weave dominant patterns within the complex tapestry of human behavior. Realizing these components is the beginning of a transformational journey and not merely a cerebral exercise. By exploring the causes of toxic conduct, we can gain a deeper knowledge of our interpersonal dynamics and shed light on their frequently dark corners.

This improved understanding serves as a bridge to true empathy rather than merely being a source of information. As we realize that a lot of toxic actions stem from unresolved grief rather than malicious intent, we can start to approach relationships with a greater level of compassion. When we acknowledge that behind the surface often lie wounded souls attempting to make their way through life, it becomes easier to show grace—both to ourselves for our mistakes and to others for their trespasses.

But acknowledgment is only the first step in a deep transformation; it is not the end in and of itself. Building on this knowledge, we can go beyond simply recognizing patterns to actively modifying them in order to promote healing and progress. The potential for happier, healthier relationships built on respect and understanding really starts to bloom at this transformative stage.

CHAPTER 3: HEALING AND RECOVERY

Sometimes getting over a bad relationship can feel like waking up from a long, scary dream. The heavy feelings, the words that do not go away, and the vivid flashbacks all add to a deep sense of chaos. For many people, like Melissa, the quiet of the night time becomes a place to play over these scary memories. As the curtain of darkness falls over them, the words of doubt, regret, and sadness get louder. This makes the way to sleep difficult and winding.

It is important to know, though, that the healing path is complicated but not impossible to find your way through. With the help of experts, the support of loved ones, and the sheer drive of the human spirit, it is not only possible to find your way through this maze, it can even change your life.

As we move forward, a change becomes clear. The path of healing changes as it goes from the first tentative steps of noticing trauma to the more sure steps of coping and rebuilding. No longer is it just about healing from the hurts of the past; it is also about building a future with a stronger sense of self-worth, identity, and relationships that are healthier and more satisfying. There will be hard times along this road, but it leads to not only recovery but also deep personal growth. It leads people to a life where scars from the past become signs of strength, resilience, and hope.

I am deeply grateful for my family and friends who have been my pillars, supporting me during, after or in between my romantic relationships. And I wish the same for you as well, as it is great to have that support system on your healing and recovery journey.

3.1 ACKNOWLEDGING AND PROCESSING PAIN

Getting out of a toxic relationship can be daunting, with all the raw pain, memories, and unresolved emotions clouding your judgment. It can feel as if you're carrying a heavy burden, much like an untreated wound that festers over time. Emotional and mental scars from such relationships can be just as persistent, if not more so.

However, ignoring this pain or burying it deep within will not foster healing. True healing begins when you courageously acknowledge and confront those overwhelming feelings and memories. By understanding and diving into the depth of your pain, you initiate the crucial process of mending your inner self.

To truly move forward, you need to recognize and understand your past. Embracing a fresh start requires you to clearly see what went wrong and comprehend the extensive impact of that toxic relationship. With this clarity, you can chart a path towards healing, understanding, and ultimately, inner peace.

Understanding the Wounds

Even though they might not be apparent, emotional and psychological traumas leave lasting marks on your psyche. The fallout from a toxic relationship frequently takes the form of a complicated emotional tapestry, with each thread signifying a distinct type of hurt, such as betrayal, lowered self-esteem, or persistent uncertainty about your own judgment. Similar to physical wounds that require attention and time to heal, these emotional scars also call for compassion, tolerance, and understanding.

The weight of these feelings can be debilitating at times, like trying to find your way through a dense forest without a visible trail. Shadows from past emotional neglect, manipulation, or betrayals might appear to go on forever. But exploring this mental forest—however dark —is essential to figuring out how to get out. Regardless of how scary these emotions may be, facing them opens the door to discovering their causes and how they affect your current situation.

The healing process really starts with this realization. Handling these feelings, recognizing where they came from and giving them the attention and room they require to heal, is similar to ministering to individual wounds. The weight starts to shift when each emotion is faced, comprehended, and processed over time, creating space for renewal, development, and a future free from the wounds of the past.

Despite its challenges, understanding and accepting past traumas can be a helpful form of self-care. Acknowledging the extent and impact of these wounds can help you to let go of them and build resilience, holding out hope for a healthier, brighter future.

The Power of Acknowledgment

When you stop running away from pain and instead face it, you find a deep strength. Admitting the deepest hurts, betrayals, and many other feelings that come up after a bad relationship can be a very life-changing experience. There are times when you probably want to avoid pain altogether, but the first step to real healing is to accept it for what it is and how it affects you. Step by step, the way to healing becomes clear when you allow yourself to grieve, get angry, think, and look for closure.

Understanding is the next step after just acknowledging something. By digging deep into your mental reserves, you can fully understand where the trauma came from. This is not about going over the past again; it is about getting clear—about the triggers, patterns, and lessons that are teaching you through the hurt. This clarity that comes from thinking about yourself is a blueprint for resilience that will help you not only recover but also get better after something bad happens.

With this new information, you can start to build a wall around your inner core to protect it. You can become better at spotting the first signs of toxic relationships, being more aware of your own limits, and avoiding situations that could affect your mental health for the worse. Talking about the bad things that happened to you in the past would help give you a stronger emotional intuition that will guide you to better, more satisfying relationships in the future.

An important part of healing is recognizing what is going on. Allow yourself to recognize that the patterns of your past do not shape your future. Make room for strength, perseverance, and newfound hope.

Embracing the Healing Process

Healing is not a straightforward process; it is more like navigating a winding path with its fair share of ups and downs. It requires a profound exploration of your core, shaped by past events and heartbreaks. Every tear you shed, every memory you revisit, and every emotion you acknowledge becomes key to your healing journey. By bravely confronting your deepest wounds, you not only remember past hurts but also start to understand their origins, the patterns they have created, and their impact on your psyche.

In navigating this terrain, you will discover an incredible resilience within yourself. While this journey is filled with emotional challenges, it is transformative. The insights you gain act as guiding beacons, ensuring every step you take leads towards growth and empowerment.

Each step, whether it is acknowledgment, thought, or change, fits together to make a whole process. This process offers not only healing from past traumas but also the birth of a new, stronger, more self-aware *you* who is ready to face a future full of love, hope, and endless possibilities.

3.2 COPING MECHANISMS AND HEALING TOOLS

Dealing with the fallout from a bad relationship can make you feel like you are lost in a big, rough sea. You might feel like waves of anger and bitterness are going to pull you under, but then waves of guilt and sadness could come in and cool you off. Emotions come and go without warning, making you feel unstable and looking for a stable base.

It makes sense that you want security and assurance in these crazy times. In the same way that a sailor looks for the lighthouse during a storm, you may be looking for ways to keep your cool and get through the mental storm. This search for mental balance is the first step on a path of self-reflection, self-care, and eventually, healing.

PROFESSIONAL GUIDANCE AND GROUNDING EXERCISES

Getting help from a professional can make a huge difference in your long and difficult road to health and healing. Therapists and counselors know how to help you find your way through the rough waters of your feelings and give you the clarity and perspective you need to move forward. Their job is to make sure that your healing is not a generic process but a path that is specific to your needs by creating strategies that are based on your specific experiences.

As part of this process, grounding techniques can become very important. Even though they are easy, they have a big effect. You can stay firmly in the present moment with grounding methods. This can be a safe place to be even when things seem to be going against you. They give you a short break, a chance to temporarily separate yourself from strong feelings or upsetting memories. With regular practice and the help of a professional, these methods go from being useful tools to being essential anchors that bring comfort and stability during rough times.

Some grounding exercises that therapists can teach you include the 5-4-3-2-1 technique, mindful breathing, body scan, guided imagery, affirmations, and others.

Journaling: An Emotional Outlet

Writing in a journal is a classic and deeply personal tool that will always be useful. This simple activity, which comes from the custom of writing down your experiences, becomes a healing activity for many people who have been through bad relationships. By expressing your feelings on paper, you have a unique chance to make your inner world visible to others, creating a physical record of your journey.

The act of putting feelings and thoughts into words is beneficial in many ways. For starters, it lets out much-needed emotional steam, which makes you feel lighter and able to breathe better. Each entry is a record of your journey as a survivor, whether it shows times when you were weak or strong. By going back through the pages over time, you can see how your healing has progressed, finding patterns, celebrating success, and learning more about problems that have not gone away.

Journal writing also helps you think about yourself. During quiet times of thought, this will often help you gain clarity by figuring out what sets off your reactions and, more importantly, by picturing a future free of the chains of past traumas. This sense of clarity can help guide your healing journey, which is why writing it down on paper is more than just a way to express yourself. It can be a source of hope and help you understand yourself better.

Meditation: Finding Inner Peace

Meditation is like a lighthouse of peace, giving your mind and soul a safe place to rest from the rough waves of life. It is not just a practice; it is a way for people who have been through bad relationships to find peace in the chaos of their feelings. Through meditation, they learn how to center themselves, keep their thoughts stable, and handle the intense emotions that might try to take over.

The steady beat of your breath, which is an important part of many types of meditation, gently brings you back to the present moment. By focusing on this breath, you are led away from the unpleasant memories of the past or the unsure future that makes you anxious. Mindfulness makes you stronger over time if you practice it regularly. Even though the emotional storms are still happening, they do not seem as scary as they used to. You will learn to find peace in the middle of the chaos.

Meditation not only calms you down right away, but it also gives you deep insights into your own mind. You can start to see trends, understand triggers, and have a compassionate conversation with yourself if you just sit with your feelings without judging them or fighting them. As well, meditation gives you the tools you need to rebuild your inner peace and keep it.

REDISCOVERING JOY THROUGH HOBBIES

Getting over a bad relationship can leave the scenery of your heart feeling empty, devoid of all its colors and life. During these times, finding old interests and hobbies again is like a gentle rain that cools the soul and brings life back to dry land. Whether it is drawing, reading, hiking, or any other favorite activity, your hobbies can be a bridge to reconnecting with the core of who you are and who you can be again.

As you do these things, you may feel temporarily moved to a different world where the weight of your past does not weigh as heavily. Every brushstroke, page turn, or step in the wild is a small act of defiance, a statement of strength and desire to find joy again. When you are deeply involved in your hobbies, you will feel some kind of peace and a confirmation that life is worth living even when it hurts.

In addition, hobbies present a lovely paradox. They let you be alone and think, but they can also help you connect with others and form communities. You can meet other people who understand what you have gone through by, for example, joining a book club, taking art classes, or going camping with a group. This helps you make connections and build networks of support. The healing process goes significantly faster in these shared places of passion and joy.

The Power of Support Networks

The real power of human connection can be your compass as you work to heal from the effects of a difficult relationship. Even though your own ways of dealing are important, the strength and shared experiences of people in your support network can often help you heal faster. Friends, family, and dedicated support groups become your rock-solid foundations, giving you not only practical help but also the comfort of knowing you understand and having been through the same thing.

Within these safe spaces, where real care and empathy rule, you can find acceptance of your emotions, validation of your experiences, and understanding of your pain. When you are with people you care about, the haunting sounds of old heartaches can fade away. People who come together can pull you up and help you, being a steady force as you try to rebuild. In the same way, hearing stories of strength and hope at support group events is a powerful way to remember that you are not alone in your battle. Sharing stories, sighs of relief, and words of support become the ties that hold everyone together, weaving a safe web of understanding and sensitivity.

The most amazing thing about these support groups is not just the comfort they give, but also the new perspectives they give. You can see examples of your own strength and the possibility of getting better in them. They strengthen the belief that healing is not only possible, but also inevitable with time, persistence, and the power of the group as a whole.

3.3 THERAPY AND COUNSELING AS SOURCES OF SUPPORT

Going through the aftermath of a breakup of a bad relationship can feel like navigating rough waters on the road to healing and recovery. Every emotion and painful memory can make it seem impossible to move on. Despite your strength and determination, you may need an anchor to hold on to when things get tough. At times like these, having the support and companionship of others can make a huge difference, as opposed to trying to get through it on your own.

Every survivor possesses a deep well of personal resilience, a core of strength that was built through challenging experiences—you just need to believe that you have that in you. Nevertheless, having the support of your loved ones can often make this inner strength even stronger. Friends and family can be like steady rocks in the middle of rough seas, providing solace, empathy, and a listening ear. However, even though this kind of support is very helpful, a more organized and professional form of support can sometimes be even better.

Here, the job of therapists and counselors really shows. These experts not only know a lot about the complicated human mind, but they also understand the unique problems that people who have been through bad relationships face. At the same time, their presence during difficult times can be a beacon of hope. They have the ability to guide you through the stormy waters towards a healthier state of mind. Their knowledge and expertise are not only helpful, but also a sign of their genuine concern for your well-being. Each interaction with them will bring you closer to healing and rediscovering your inner strength and resilience.

The Role of Therapists and Counselors

In the past—or in some cases, even in the present—there was a certain stigma surrounding seeing therapists and counselors. Seeing therapists was perceived as a weakness or failure, with the belief that you should be able to handle your problems on your own. This belief contributed to feelings of shame and inadequacy. Another one was that in certain cultures or social cultures, openly discussing mental health or seeking professional help was not seen as the norm, which in turn created barriers for fear of judgment or discrimination from their community. Gender stereotypes also played a role, with some individuals, especially men, feeling societal pressure to appear strong and self-reliant. Seeking help was perceived as a deviation from traditional gender roles.

Thankfully, in these present times, these stigmas are being challenged and dismantled through education about the benefits, normalizing mental health discussions, and sharing stories of recovery. It is still your choice, but I must emphasize that seeking therapy is a courageous and positive step you can take toward healing.

Therapists and counselors play many parts in the healing process. They are there to listen, give advice, and help show you the way. With years of training and a lot of experience, they are able to offer tools and methods that are specific to your needs. A therapist can help you make sense of the storm of emotions that might be coming up and how to deal with them—whether stress, anger, guilt, or any other feelings you may have.

In addition, therapy meetings provide a structured setting that acts as a safe haven bound by confidentiality, a place of peace and understanding where you can talk freely without fear of being judged. This is where you can learn how to deal with everyday problems and regain control over your life again.

It is important to note that you should discuss confidentiality with your therapist or counselor at the beginning of your therapeutic relationship to understand the specific policies and legal or ethical limitations. Clear communication about confidentiality helps build trust between you and your therapist or counselor and ensures that you are aware of the circumstances under which they may be obligated to breach confidentiality, just in case.

Dealing with the Shadows of Narcissistic Relationships

You may feel like you are going through a maze where the walls are always moving. Having these kinds of relationships casts long, often elusive shadows, which makes the way to healing complicated and hard. The harm is not just on the surface; it goes deep, digging up holes of self-doubt, eroding the foundation of your sense of self-worth, and changing how you see love, trust, and closeness. Even though these wounds are deep, they are sometimes hard to see, which makes them even more sneaky and hard to heal.

Therapy programs designed for individuals who have experienced narcissistic relationships delve deeper into the psychological scars left behind, rather than just the visible ones. Therapists help you figure out and unpack the patterns of manipulation you were exposed to and endured. It is a process of rediscovery. The increased awareness acquired through this process can help you differentiate between real love and manipulation, ultimately rebuilding your sense of self-worth one step at a time.

When you get out of a narcissistic situation, you have to set new limits for yourself. You can learn to set strong, clear limits with the help of a professional, which protects you from future manipulation. Somewhat like a rebirth—a change from a caterpillar stuck in a cocoon of old memories to a butterfly, ready to take on new journeys with new knowledge, strength, and a stronger sense of who you are.

Moving Forward with Renewed Strength

The path to healing and recovery is both complicated and unique to each person. It is a journey that calls you to face your fears, relieve your pain, and find lost parts of yourself again. But you do not have to be alone on this journey of self-reflection. There are a lot of resources available to you as we have already covered, whether it is the unwavering support of family and friends, the wise advice of experts, or the immense strength of your own spirit.

Leaning into these places of support and strength makes the often overwhelming process of healing easier to handle. Every act of understanding, every therapy session, and every time you think about yourself is like a stepping stone that makes the next step easier to see and less scary.

These tools, both inside and outside of you, heal emotional wounds, slowly putting together broken pieces to give your soul a new life.

When you come out of this process, you can proudly wear your scars—not to remember the hurt you've been through, but to show how strong and wise you are. The ordeal, which used to be painful, is now a sign of your unbreakable spirit, your deeper knowledge of yourself, and your growing awareness of how complicated human relationships are. With these new insights and skills, you can move forward, ready to face the world with renewed energy and a firm belief that you can overcome obstacles.

3.4 EMBRACING SELF-CARE: NURTURING YOUR SELF

Getting out of a bad relationship can be very hard and leave you feeling very tired. It is hard on both the mind and the heart when you are upset or stressed. It is a lot like getting through a rough storm—you feel lost and like everything you do and think is fragile, and you want to find a place of peace and understanding.

After going through such a rough time, the natural response might be to look for outside approval or something to do. But the real way to get better often starts with looking inside. This trip into self-reflection is more than just a way to heal; it is a lifeline that leads to your true self. During these critical times, self-care is no longer just a trendy phrase but has become a fundamental part of healing.

Taking care of yourself is a conscious act of love and self-preservation. It gives you a solid base from which you can begin to fix your broken spirit. Through nurturing practices, you can slowly but surely heal your mental wounds and feel at peace with yourself again. As this base gets stronger, the way forward becomes clearer, thanks to the new light of self-awareness and compassion.

PHYSICAL ACTIVITIES AS A BALM

After a bad relationship or trauma, the healing process makes the deep link between the body and mind even clearer. As your journey continues, physical exercise not only is a necessary habit but also an important way to heal. Each step you take on your morning walk, each deep breath you take during yoga, or each beat of your gym workout becomes proof of your body's ability to heal and grow.

Endorphins are chemicals that make you feel good. Just moving your body gets them released. People often call these biochemicals "nature's antidote to pain" because they are so good at reducing stress and improving happiness. There is a deeper, more profound side to this than just the instant physical benefits. When you do physical activities on a daily basis, they become a ritual, a set time when you put your health first. This is a strong, quiet way to show that you are still committed and that you deserve care and attention.

The spirit also gets stronger and more flexible when you work out regularly, just like your body does. The discipline, commitment, and small wins that come from these physical activities are like the bigger journey of recovery. Each workout finished or goal reached becomes a symbol, showing progress in healing your soul, regaining your self-worth, and building strength for you to face life's challenges.

MINDFULNESS: THE ANCHOR TO THE PRESENT

When you have been through a bad relationship, your mind can be very unstable, with memories of the bad relationship coming back to you, and you have doubts about the future. At this moment, practicing awareness is of the utmost importance. It is a place of peace in the middle of an inner storm, a way to get across the rough waters of tumultuous feelings and thoughts and reach a plateau of peace and self-connection. When you practice mindfulness, every deep breath you take is like a whisper of comfort, and every moment of stillness is like a gentle reminder of your own inner power.

Mindfulness is a journey that offers much more than just a practice. It is a gentle and caring walk that takes you to the present moment, where the noise of your thoughts and the chaos of the outside world cease for a while. Returning to yourself through mindfulness is a sacred act that can bring healing and inner peace. When achieved, the moments of silence can provide a peaceful haven where healing energies can flow freely.

This safe place gives the wounds caused by bad relationships room to breathe. Getting in touch with the rhythms of the present moment frees you from the chains of past tragedies and worries about the future. Every time you practice mindfulness, you are taking a step toward freedom, moving gracefully away from the loud sounds of toxic relationships toward the beautiful music of self-connection and inner peace.

Setting Boundaries: The Art of Prioritization

Setting clear personal limits is often necessary to get through the rough times that follow the end of a bad relationship. Self-care can be more than just physical activities and quiet reflection for some people. It can also involve setting and maintaining boundaries. This is particularly important if you have experienced manipulation and control. Setting limits is not only about determining what is acceptable and what is not, but it also demonstrates your worth and independence. Saying "no" firmly but gracefully is not a sign of weakness or incompetence. Instead, it is a clear indication of your newfound self-awareness and inner strength.

Setting these limits goes beyond just talking to other people. You can protect your emotional and mental space in a lot of different ways. This action is not so much about keeping other people out as it is about caring for what is inside you—keeping the healing process safe and making sure that personal time, space, and energy are valued and appreciated. Setting boundaries is like building a brick wall of self-respect. It shows the world, but most importantly yourself, how much you value your health and peace of mind.

It is important to set limits and prioritize self-care, as it can have a significant impact on your life. By taking care of yourself, you can reconnect with your inner self and show yourself love, respect, and kindness, even during difficult times. This lesson is learned in moments of quiet reflection when we feel the beating of our own hearts. Self-care not only helps us prepare for recovery, but it also gives us hope, strength, and a sense of self-respect. Survivors of toxic relationships, in particular, understand the importance of these practices and principles, and they can serve as a guiding light of hope, strength, and self-respect.

CHAPTER 4: REBUILDING SELF-ESTEEM AND CONFIDENCE

*M*elissa stood still for a moment, her eyes locked onto the figure staring back at her from the mirror. The features she once admired were now overshadowed by a barrage of criticisms, each one echoing the harsh words of her former toxic partner. Those criticisms, once external, had insidiously made their way into her internal narrative, distorting the way she viewed herself. Every perceived flaw, every minor imperfection, was magnified, obscuring the beauty and strength that lay beneath.

The journey to self-recovery is not easy, but with the right tools, strategies, and understanding, it is a path that leads to a destination filled with promise and potential. As someone who has gone through a toxic relationship, you may often face challenges related to your sense of self-worth, confidence, and self-esteem. There are a lot of "self-" terms that capture your feelings, thoughts, and actions towards yourself and it is natural if these terms seem to blur together, but each carries distinct meanings, implications, and purposes.

The most vital "self-" concept of all is self-worth (Ackerman, 2018). Your self-worth is not based on your relationship, especially a toxic relationship. Someone else's love, or lack of love for that matter, does not determine your value as a person, whether you are single, casually dating, in a developing relationship, or celebrating decades with your spouse. Regardless of your relationship status, it is important to recognize your inherent worth and prioritize self-acceptance and self-compassion.

As you tread this path of self-recovery, you will find that rebuilding self-esteem is just the beginning. In order to do that, you must know your self-worth—you are worthy to be your own person and you can take the steps to find that confidence in you even if you currently feel lost and down. With a newfound sense of confidence and assurance as your bedrock, you will be better equipped to navigate the next crucial phase of healing: the establishment of healthy boundaries, which we will cover in the next chapter. This pivotal skill, once mastered, serves as a guardian of your self-worth and a protector of your emotional well-being, ensuring that the progress you make is not only maintained but also continually nurtured.

4.1 REDISCOVERING SELF-WORTH

When you are going through something mentally draining, like a toxic relationship, doubt can make it hard to see how brilliant you really are. As a result of constant criticism and putting yourself down, this fog often forms. Each word or action weakens your once-strong sense of self-worth, sending you into a downward spiral.

But there is an unshakable truth about you that is waiting to come through this thick fog of bad ideas. No matter the problems or losses you have been through, you have value in and of yourself. This inner power and uniqueness is what makes you stand out, no matter what other people think or what is going on around you.

When you feel low self-worth and doubt, it is important to remember that these are only brief feelings. They might temporarily lessen your shine, but they cannot take it away. You can peel back these layers to rediscover and accept your true, natural worth if you are strong, honest, and love yourself.

Keep in mind that your self-worth and value as a person is not determined by your attractiveness, financial status, or your social status. While the pursuit of money, status, and popularity is top of mind for many people in society, take a step back and reflect on what genuinely matters in assessing people's worth: kindness, compassion, empathy, respect for others, and how you treat those around you.

As well, you can focus on recognizing, challenging, and externalizing your inner critic who is always eager to highlight your flaws. It is natural that this voice may affect you occasionally, but do not let it win too often. Take a pause and question whether the voice's observations are factual, kind, or necessary. If not, feel empowered to toss it out the door!

The Impact of Toxicity on Self-worth

A toxic relationship can make you feel bad about who you are for a long time. Every insulting word or look acts like a poison drop, slowly fading the bright colors of your confidence and self-esteem. When bad things keep happening to you, you might start to doubt your own abilities over time. What used to be a clear, positive picture of yourself gets bent and warped into something strange and mean.

This constant negative can slowly take root in your mind as the days turn into weeks and months. This is the risk of absorbed negativity: when you start to mix up your negative thoughts with positive ones, the line between the two starts to blur. As damaging stories start to take over your mind instead of just coming from outside sources, it may be hard to tell the difference between these forced distortions and your true self.

This is how poisonous things work: they are sneaky. They do not just show up in words or deeds that are obvious. When they get into your mind, they can make you doubt your own worth and replace your self-belief with a

CHAPTER 4: REBUILDING SELF-ESTEEM AND CONFIDE... | 69

skewed standard based on unfair criticism and comments from other people.

THE JOURNEY OF SELF-APPRECIATION

Regaining your sense of self-worth is like setting out on a deep introspective journey, a voyage to the inner sanctuary of your heart. It is a conscious decision to take a moment to stop, turn away from the noise outside, and adopt a more loving, caring perspective of yourself. This reflective journey is about more than just counting accomplishments; it is about realizing the worth that lies in each and every action, every obstacle overcome, and every lesson discovered.

Any and every accomplishment you have, no matter how big or small, serves as evidence of your fortitude, tenacity, and development as a person. No matter how anything turns out, putting in a lot of work into something shows how persistent and committed you are. It is important to realize that the journey itself, with all of its highs and lows, is just as important as any destination. Your story becomes richer and more complex with each hurdle and detour.

However, there is another kind of appreciation that goes beyond accomplishments and hard work: accepting and appreciating your individuality. Each person adds a unique combination of traits, insights, and life experiences to the mosaic of existence. Acknowledging and valuing your uniqueness—this unique concoction of your characteristics and experiences—becomes essential to constructing a renewed and strong sense of self-worth.

INTRINSIC VALUE: UNALTERED AND UNALTERABLE

Every person has an underlying, constant truth that is important to who they are: their intrinsic value. Your value as a person does not change with social norms or life's unpredictable events. Rather, it remains a steady reminder of self-worth. It is not influenced by criticism or judgment from other people.

Realizing this great truth can be transformational. You need to tune into the constant symphony of your own value and rise above the clatter of outside validations and criticisms. Even though happy and difficult life experiences can sculpt your character, affect your self-esteem, and change your image of yourself, these outside influences just scratch the surface. Below these exterior layers is the foundation of your indisputable worth.

Accepting this empowering viewpoint becomes an important turning point in your life. It represents a deep realization that your worth is unquestionable and independent of approval from others. You possess an inborn gem that is timeless and priceless, and you deserve respect, admiration, and firm confidence in yourself.

This process of rediscovering your value is definitely a journey that entails removing the layers of societal expectations, past traumas, and external judgments in order to reveal your true self underneath.

A stronger sense of identity—a grasp of your abilities, interests, and distinctive qualities that characterize yourself—emerges with each step down this journey. This fresh understanding not only boosts self-esteem but also serves as a compass, pointing you in the direction of decisions and connections that are authentically you. It turns into an inner light that chases away the doubt and insecurity that may have previously obscured your judgment.

This newly established sense of self-worth establishes the groundwork for your life going forward that is full of significance and purpose. As mutual respect and understanding are the foundation of a relationship, it becomes more authentic. Your decisions and choices become more in line with your goals and ideals. Regaining your sense of self-worth allows you to create a future filled with contentment, happiness, and unshakeable belief in yourself.

4.2 IDENTIFYING AND CHALLENGING NEGATIVE SELF-TALK

Within the depths of our minds, there is a persistent voice that keeps shouting. It often arises during moments of peace, like an unwelcome guest, whispering comments full of doubt, criticism, and belittlement. These mental echoes, the haunting remnants of a harmful past, keep repeating themselves, gradually eroding the self-esteem and confidence that we strive so hard to build.

The inner dialogues that you may experience can be a result of past interactions that have left you feeling unworthy. However, it is important to realize that these negative thoughts are, once again, not a reflection of your true worth. By acknowledging and challenging them, it is possible to overcome the self-defeating dialogue and start viewing yourself in a more positive light. Remember, even the most glorious occasions can be tarnished by doubt, but with self-awareness and self-compassion, it is possible to rise above it and discover your true value.

Recognizing the Inner Critic

The inner critic frequently takes center stage, offering uninvited criticism and exaggerating every perceived error. But the first step in destroying its power is to draw attention to it, identify its trends, and comprehend its history. This calls for your conscious reflection and deliberate pauses to pay attention to the things that are running through your mind, particularly when you are feeling vulnerable, introspective, or faced with difficulties.

Ask yourself: *Are these ideas constantly beset with criticism? Is it a tendency to downplay my own accomplishments while magnifying any small mistake I make?*

It may come as a surprise to you that the inner conversations you have with yourself on a regular basis can have a significant impact on how you perceive yourself and your beliefs. Identifying these conversations requires more than just passive awareness. You need to actively take note of the recurring stories, understand the situations in which they arise, and pinpoint the emotional triggers that amplify their frequency.

Look and think inwardly and you can identify and recognize the critic within you. This is the first step towards reclaiming control of your thoughts and emotions. Even though you acknowledge its presence, you can ensure that your self-worth and identity are no longer defined by its influence.

Challenging and Reframing the Narrative

Identifying and examining negative self-talk patterns is only the first step of a lengthy mental transformation process. Once you have uncovered these tendencies, you must take the next step on the more challenging yet incredibly transformative journey of questioning and modifying these narratives. Simply acknowledging these unwanted thoughts is not enough; actively scrutinizing, challenging, and analyzing them helps reduce their grip on your mind and emotions.

You should stop and consider, *Is this truly what I believe about myself, or is this a distorted reflection of past experiences or external opinions?* when confronted with the voice of your inner critic. Sometimes, you may tend to find yourself making self-deprecating statements. However, these statements may not be an actual reflection of your true self. Instead, they may have been influenced by negative experiences in your past relationships. It is important to reflect and identify whether these thoughts stem from a genuine self-evaluation or whether they have been influenced by external criticism. When you understand the origin of these thoughts, it will empower you to reframe your mindset and overcome harmful beliefs.

In cases where you face a challenge that seems insurmountable, you can overcome your negative thoughts by recalling your past successes and assets. Although it may be difficult, this process will help you adjust your perspective and replace negative self-talk with a compassionate and accurate way of viewing yourself. It is about rediscovering your true voice and ensuring that it speaks louder than the lingering effects of past negativity. With this thinking process, you can conquer any obstacle and live your best life.

4.3 PRACTICING SELF-COMPASSION AND SELF-LOVE

Healing involves being kind to yourself, and that is where self-compassion plays a vital role. Self-compassion is different from self-esteem, which is based on judgments and comparisons. It does not require you to be perfect or superior. Instead, it is about showing understanding and being gentle with yourself, especially during challenging times or when things do not go as planned. It is like having a small voice inside you that comforts you when you feel vulnerable or insecure. This knowledge is what helps you realize that everyone faces obstacles and has flaws, regardless of their background or situation. You have to recognize that the challenges you face are simply a part of life, rather than a reflection of incompetence or inadequacy.

Taking Up Self-Love

Self-love involves intentionally practicing activities that praise and honor yourself, while self-compassion involves empathy and understanding. It means making a conscious decision to prioritize your happiness and well-being. This can be as simple as taking some time out during a busy day, revisiting a beloved hobby, or pursuing activities that bring you joy and enthusiasm. It is about making choices that demonstrate consideration, respect, and deep gratitude for yourself.

If you want to delve deeper into the topic of self-love, you can also read one of my other books, *The Self-Love Path: How to Embrace Self-Compassion and Kindness to Yourself and Achieve Your Goals*, if you haven't read it already.

Daily Gratitude Exercises

Daily affirmations are essential to this path of self-love and compassion because they are strong declarations of your own value, worth, and competence. By consistently affirming your intrinsic value, you can strengthen your belief in yourself. The power of repetition, whether it is writing positive statements in a journal or standing in front of a mirror and declaring, "I am enough," can transform how you think and replace self-doubt with confidence and self-belief.

The practices of self-love and self-compassion are essential for healing, not just mere buzzwords. By combining positive actions and understanding, you can effectively rebuild your damaged self-image and develop a loving, respectful, and compassionate relationship with yourself —and consequently, with others.

4.4 BUILDING HEALTHY HABITS AND ROUTINES

Often overlooked, a routine can be your anchor in the unpredictable tides of life. And in this rapidly changing world, where nothing stays the same for long, where unexpected challenges and demands can easily throw you off balance, the consistency of a well-structured routine offers you stability. It is more than just a to-do list or a scheduled day; it is a grounding force, granting you a semblance of control in your daily life.

When you intentionally craft and stick to such a routine, you lay a solid foundation for yourself. This structure, subtle yet powerful, becomes a sanctuary of reassurance, diminishing anxiety and acting as a shield from life's pressures. When working within a structured framework, setting and achieving goals can have a transformative effect. These goals, regardless of their size, have a dual purpose. They offer you direction, ensuring that each day of yours has a purpose and meaning. Additionally, every accomplishment, no matter how big or small, serves as a personal affirmation. Celebrating these victories helps to boost your self-esteem and fuels your motivation to keep moving forward.

In essence, adopting a routine is about carving out a space where you can thrive, gain clarity, and continually tap into your potential. It is not just about organization; it is about empowerment.

Passion-aligned Activities

Engaging in things that are a deep fit with your inner passions is like drawing from a source of purpose, fulfillment, and joy. These are deeper manifestations of your spirit and are reflections of your deepest aspirations and inclinations; more than just hobbies or interests. Painting, writing, dancing, or any other number of endeavors are not merely behaviors; they are affirmations of your intrinsic qualities and talents.

Each paintbrush stroke on a canvas, each written phrase, each rhythmic movement, all serve as a testimonial to the artist's ability. They act as potent reminders of the distinct combination of abilities, aptitudes, and viewpoints that each person possesses. Apart from the happiness you get when doing these kinds of activities, they consistently enhance your self-worth. They provide you with concrete proof of your imagination, tenacity, and unique contribution to the world.

For me, writing is one of my passions. It doesn't even necessarily mean that you have to be the best at doing it. What matters is that you have the passion for it. There are so many different areas that you can explore. For example, to explore your creative side—you can paint, write poetry or stories, play a musical instrument, or crocheting. If you like outdoor activities—you can hike in nature, do nature photography, do gardening, go rock climbing, or other outdoor sports. If you like learning and education—you can join a book club, learn a new language, or pursue online courses or certifications. If you like to be engaged in the community—you can volunteer for a cause, organize or participate in community events, support marginalized communities, and others.

It is a world of endless possibilities! Engaging in passion-driven pursuits is about more than just enjoying yourself. It is an amazing journey of discovering your true self and recognizing your worth that leads to a never-ending celebration of your unique abilities.

Prioritizing Physical Well-being

The relationship between mental and physical health is complex and multifaceted. Taking care of your body is an enduring commitment to yourself, not just an exercise regimen. If you regularly exercise—whether it is through a yoga class, an energizing morning jog, or a leisurely stroll in the park—you are doing more than just working out your body. You are releasing a massive amount of endorphins, which are nature's happy-makers and uplifters.

Adding a healthy diet to your physical activity increases the advantages. Eating a diet full of vital nutrients nourishes your mind in addition to your body. Eating the appropriate foods can improve your memory, improve your cognitive performance, and reduce any mood swings. When you make eating healthy food choices a priority, you are communicating to yourself that you value your overall health and well-being.

By combining mindful eating with regular exercise, you can establish a strong basis for self-care. This proactive approach improves your spirit and fortifies your body. It turns into a never-ending confirmation of your value as a person, highlighting the conviction that you are worthy of the best health and happiness life has to offer.

Dedicated "Me-time"

It is imperative that you set out specific time for yourself. These deliberate breaks from the noise of everyday responsibilities and chores are havens of comfort. Now is the perfect moment to get back in touch with yourself, whether that means curling up with a favorite book, taking a peaceful bath, or just spending some quiet time alone in thought.

This "me-time" is a meaningful act of self-affirmation rather than merely a break. When you value these times of reflection and alone time, you are sending a strong message to yourself: *I matter.* Your happiness, goals, and general well-being are all worthwhile and worthy of consideration.

These short yet meaningful breaks can have a significant and enduring impact. They rejuvenate your mind, allowing for introspection and comprehension. They also fortify your spirit by serving as a continuous reminder of your innate worth and the importance of self-care in the face of life's numerous challenges.

Surrounding Yourself with Positivity

Your mentality is greatly influenced by the people and environments you are exposed to. Creating a positive atmosphere for yourself by surrounding yourself with understanding and helpful people, reading books on inspiration, or listening to uplifting music, serves as a barrier against negativity. Not only does this uplifting environment provide regular reinforcement of messages of resilience, self-worth, and potential, but it also uplifts the spirit.

Developing healthy routines and habits is a holistic way to take care of your body, mind, and soul—it is not just about organization or discipline. By intentionally incorporating these components into your daily life, you are able to build a strong basis for improved self-worth, self-assurance, and a life that is full of positivity and meaning.

CHAPTER 5: ESTABLISHING HEALTHY BOUNDARIES

Melissa was at a turning point as she dealt with the upheaval that followed the end of her toxic relationship. The events, which were both scary and eye-opening, gave her a choice. She could either stay stuck in the effects of emotional horrors from the past, or she could seize the moment to start a new path toward independence and emotional safety. Melissa realized how important it is to set and stick to limits after reflecting on her own experiences and attaining clarity.

Boundaries are the unseen lines that separate your emotional, physical, and mental spaces. They are often a mix of art and science. In the shadows of relationships that are harmful, these lines often get fuzzy or disappear. You can change them, strengthen them, and value them, as we will see in this chapter.

5.1 THE POWER OF "NO"

It is amazing how powerful a simple two-letter word can be: "No". This short answer is more than just a negative at its core. It is an agreement about what you stand for, your limits, and your borders. For many, especially those who have grown up in unhealthy situations, just saying this one word can be like pulling out all the stops. But when used wisely, "no" can be a barrier that keeps you from situations that could drain your emotional reserves or lead you down roads that are full of pain or conflict.

When you leave a relationship where your wishes were often ignored or where your boundaries were often crossed, the act of saying "no" goes beyond its direct meaning. It becomes a symbol of regaining your independence and a sign of how much you value and respect yourself. Getting comfortable with this word can be hard because of feelings that come up inside, but it is an important step to take to protect your emotional and mental health.

I must admit that I have had trouble saying no to things myself. This applied to both my personal and professional life. Eventually, with the encouragement from my mentors, I slowly learned to be more comfortable in saying no to other people when I allowed myself to recognize my limitations.

It is important to know, though, that the power of "no" doesn't come from being stubborn or defiant. It comes from being self-aware and wanting to protect yourself. Being aware of situations that go against your core values or that could cause you mental or physical stress and being assertive about them will keep you from being overworked or forced into situations you do not want to be in. In the big picture of relationships and contacts with other people, being able to say "no" sets the stage for fair, open, and honest conversations.

5.2 EFFECTIVE COMMUNICATION FOR HEALTHY BOUNDARIES

Effective communication is crucial in human interactions. Personal boundaries play a significant role in this, and they are more than mere safety nets. You need to communicate clearly and articulate your boundaries to ensure that others respect them. You, me, everyone—we all have limits, and you need to recognize that you need space to grow in different aspects of your life. Therefore, setting boundaries involves informing others of those limits.

Conversing effectively goes beyond just talking to each other. There is a fine line between being bold about your wants and needs and making sure that your message is understood and respected. To do this, you need to work on skills like active listening, which means being fully present in the conversation and responding in a way that shows you understand and agree with the other person. The goal of this dialogue process is to develop a shared knowledge in which everyone feels heard, understood, and valued.

However, conversation is not just reactive or defensive when it comes to setting boundaries. It is proactive and aims to create a space where you can succeed without always worrying about upstepping or being stepped on. Setting clear limits and communicating them well builds trust and equal respect in your relationship, whether it is with a partner, family, friends, or people that you work with. This makes it possible for you and the other person to get to know each other better and builds a base where everyone can grow.

5.3 LAYING THE FOUNDATIONS: HOW TO SET BOUNDARIES

Setting limits requires a lot of self-awareness and talking to other people. To do this, you have to go deep into your soul and figure out what really matters at the core. This self-reflection is very important because it sets the ground rules for everything else. You can build a life that is real and full of self-respect by getting to know your core values, accepting your natural limits, and figuring out the parts of your life that you cannot change.

But looking inside is just the start of this process. When you have a clear understanding of your boundaries, it empowers you to communicate with others in an authentic and purposeful way through your actions and conversations, while inspiring those around you to do the same. It means incorporating these limits into your daily life and making sure that others notice and accept them. These methods connect your deepest beliefs with how you act in the world so you can live a life where your values are not only seen but also respected:

- **Self-awareness:** Reflect on past experiences to identify what feels uncomfortable or draining.
- **Clarity:** Be specific about what your boundaries are to avoid ambiguity.
- **Consistency:** It is essential to be consistent in maintaining boundaries to ensure they are respected.

5.4 ENFORCING BOUNDARIES

Setting boundaries is important because it communicates your beliefs, needs, and limits. However, simply mapping out your boundaries is only the beginning. To maintain the integrity of these boundaries, you must be vigilant and consistent with your discipline. Even the most carefully drawn boundaries can be violated, ignored, or disregarded if they are not consistently reinforced.

It is often more challenging to stick to the boundaries you set than it is to establish them in the first place. To do so, you must be brave, bold, and consistent. By being firm about a limit, you not only demonstrate its importance but also foster a culture of respect and understanding between yourself and others. The choices and actions that come with setting and adhering to boundaries are crucial because they ensure that these limits are respected in all of your interactions and relationships.

- **Regular check-ins:** Periodically review and, if necessary, adjust your boundaries.
- **Seek support:** Sometimes, it is beneficial to have allies who understand and support your boundaries, be it friends, family, or support groups.
- **Be assertive:** If boundaries are overstepped, it is essential that you address the issue directly and firmly.

5.5 THE BIGGER PICTURE: SELF-CARE AND BOUNDARIES

In essence, boundaries mean making a deep promise to yourself. They are more than just rules for what is okay and not okay; they are a physical sign of self-respect and self-care. These invisible screens watch over the safe places in our minds, hearts, and bodies. They serve as reminders that amidst all of life's responsibilities and relationships, there is still a sacred place that is only for your own well-being. You can take the time to recharge, do things that make you happy, and keep your emotions in check in this place.

In addition, these lines have two purposes. They do protect you from harm, but they also help you grow. Their presence makes it possible to learn from past mistakes, particularly ones that were harmful, and turn those lessons into wisdom. Setting clear limits can help you see the problems and difficulties you have had in the past in a new way, turning them into stepping stones that lead to more caring, balanced, and mutually respectful relationships in the future.

By setting boundaries, you are taking an important step towards prioritizing your well-being. I must again emphasize that it is not enough to simply set them—you must also consistently reinforce them. Like a castle protected by watchful guards, these boundaries serve as a powerful symbol of your commitment to your own health and happiness. With each reinforcement, you are sending a message that you value yourself and your needs above all else.

After going over the complicated parts of setting and keeping limits and boundaries, you are now ready to go into another deep part of healing: forgiving and moving on. Even though these things are hard, they hold the key to real inner peace and are the end of a path that leads to healing and peace all over.

CHAPTER 6: FORGIVENESS AND CLOSURE

Melissa had to deal with the weight of unanswered feelings and pain that came from the memories of her troubled past. Her heart was heavy from the memories of a bad relationship, and she was looking for comfort and freedom. She quickly understood that the deep acts of forgiving and letting go were essential to her healing. These were not just words; they were strong processes, and each one had its own essence that could help her feel free emotionally.

The following are a couple of other stories on *The Forgiveness Project* by survivors who have rebuilt their lives following hurt and trauma, which I thought were worth resharing.

Ruchi Singh is a domestic violence survivor who lives in India. After she and her then-husband got married, she moved with him to Sydney, Australia. In the beginning, her husband treated her well, but then soon realized that she married a man who lost his temper easily, would use foul language, and eventually became physically violent with her, even almost getting killed by him with a knife to her throat. After surviving all that she had been through and even when her ex never apologized, she said, "Forgiveness doesn't mean saying I'm OK with what he did; it means I can continue with my life in a more peaceful frame of mind." Ruchi's experience has led her to focus her work as a speaker, mentor, talk show host, and author to promote courage and leadership for all victims.

Next is Christopher Emmanuel's story. As a child growing up in a small town in Grenada, West Indies, Christopher experienced merciless shame from his father in front of his peers. He had painful memories from the young age of 7 as he was made to kneel on a steel grate cover in front of an open door while naked, while at the same time enduring the mocking laughter of the neighborhood kids passing by. That was only one of the many hurtful experiences he had in his childhood including the years when he and his family moved to and lived in Toronto, Canada. He felt unsafe with his father, and this affected all his relationships as time went on. He suppressed the anger, which several years later led to mental illness. After a decade of struggles in and out of institutions, he was able to heal and explore forgiveness with his father. He said, "Forgiveness took away the illusion that my past had made me powerless. It rekindled my faith in a higher power, strengthened my sense of morality, and created a totally new reality." Christopher is now a counsellor and he teaches the power of forgiveness.

A lot of people find that time alone is not enough to fix them. It requires the soul's grace, which means being ready to forgive not only the people who hurt you but also yourself for any flaws or weaknesses you think you have. To forgive someone, you have to search inward to let go of your anger and bitterness. In the same way, closure acts as a beacon of clarity that signals the end of scenes that no longer belong in the story of your life.

6.1 UNDERSTANDING THE ESSENCE OF FORGIVENESS

Forgiving someone is, at its core, a deep act of freedom. Not only is it about forgiving someone for their mistakes, but it is also about freeing yourself from the fire of hatred, anger, and bitterness. If you hold on to this emotional turmoil, it turns into a never-ending loop that brings up hurt feelings and perceived betrayals, slowly eroding your peace of mind and sense of self-worth.

When we talk about forgiveness, we need to understand that it has two sides. On one hand, it means showing understanding and kindness to people who have hurt you, looking at them through a lens that tries to see past their hurtful actions to see if there are deeper reasons or weaknesses. Also, and this may be more important, it is about showing yourself the same kindness. Understand that carrying around unresolved anger and pain is like carrying a heavy load that limits your emotional freedom and growth.

As a result, real forgiveness is not just an action; it is a journey within yourself. It is about looking for the strength to break free from the ties of the past and finding it. Realizing that some things in life might not change, but how you react to them can. It is possible to heal, make peace, and grow when you choose to forgive.

6.2 THE MISCONCEPTIONS SURROUNDING FORGIVENESS

I completely understand that forgiveness can be a difficult and complex process; I've been there. It calls us to face the shadows of our past and the echoes of hurt and anger. However, even if forgiveness can be a powerful tool for healing and finding inner peace, it is indeed a personal journey that may be different for everyone. Additionally, some people tend to have the wrong idea about true forgiveness, leaving them to struggle.

A lot of times, these misunderstandings cause fear, which makes people hesitant to go down this road because they think that forgiving might mean forgetting past mistakes or not feeling the weight of their pain. Unfortunately, these wrong ideas take away from the deep power of forgiveness, which is not about approving of someone else's actions but about freeing the forgiven person.

To truly heal, it is necessary to sort through these myths and understand what forgiveness really means. If you believe some of these misconceptions to be true, do not worry; we all make mistakes. The important thing is that you now will have a better understanding moving forward. By taking away the mystery of what it is, you can really understand its worth and use its power to make peace with your past and, more importantly, with yourself.

Forgiveness Is Not Condonation

Many people have the wrong idea that forgiving someone means tolerating or ignoring the harm they caused. Many people do not let forgiveness heal them because they are afraid that if they do, they will make the wrongs done to them seem less important or real. This is not at all what it seems to be. At its deepest level, forgiveness is not an outward validation but an improvement on the inside.

It is very important to understand that forgiving someone does not make the pain less serious. It is not a cover that hides hurtful actions or lets the person who hurts you off the hook for the choices they make. Instead, it is more like a personal release—an act that frees you from the chains of anger, hate, and hurtful memories that keep coming back to you.

Forgiving someone is also a gift to yourself; it is a way to give yourself the peace and quiet that comes from letting go of the past. Choosing to put your emotional and mental health ahead of holding on to bad feelings is an act of self-care. The act is transformative not because it changes the past or starts over for the wrongdoer, but because it changes the future, making room for mental renewal and real inner peace.

When you understand the difference between forgiving someone and condoning what they did, you can start on a real path to healing. Your choice to forgive is a sign of how strong and resilient you are, not a surrender to the wrongs of the past.

Forgiveness Does Not Mean Legal Pardon

Sometimes it seems like the sentiments people have can overlap with the rules of the legal system. This is especially true when considering the idea of forgiveness and how it relates to a pardon in court. It is important to understand that these are two separate things with different goals and roles.

Emotions, sentiments, and inner well-being are very personal areas where forgiveness is involved. Forgiveness allows you to let go of hatred, rage, or bitterness. This emotional release is not dependent on the decisions or actions of others, nor is it affected by the resolution of legal matters. Making this very personal choice can help you regain harmony and serenity and stop the past from casting a shadow over the present.

A legal pardon, on the other hand, refers to the official release from the consequences of a crime or transgression. Holding people accountable for their acts, it operates under the social frameworks of justice and accountability. Although a formal pardon may release a person from some legal repercussions, it may not always be in line with the survivor's emotional journey.

To put it another way, even while you may choose to forgive the offender on a personal level, this does not necessarily mean that you want them to be free from legal consequences. These two processes highlight how societal justice and personal healing must coexist in harmony. They reaffirm the idea that you can fervently support justice and accountability in the outside world while still fiercely desiring inner peace through forgiveness.

Forgiveness is Different from Reconciliation

If you want to find your way through forgiveness and reconciliation, it is like walking along two separate roads that don't always meet. Both processes have deep roots in the emotional range of people, but they have different goals and results.

Forgiveness is a deep journey of the soul. It is a choice to free yourself from the weight of anger, hate, and the haunting memories of past hurts. To protect yourself, you must make the choice to keep past wrongs from harming your present and future. Allowing yourself to heal, rise above the pain, and regain inner peace is what forgiveness is all about, not removing memories or lessening the effects of harm.

Getting back together with someone after a fight or breakup is what reconciliation is all about. To do it, both parties need to work together, understand each other, and often want to repair trust. Forgiveness is a very personal choice that can happen on its own, but reconciliation depends on both parties being ready and committed to it. Building bridges, re-establishing ties, and encouraging mutual respect are all part of it.

That being said, it is important to stress that forgiveness can help lead to healing, but the two are not naturally linked. It is possible to fully accept someone and find inner peace and closure without feeling like you have to make things right or start dating again. It is important to know the difference between these two terms so that on your way to mental healing you do not end up back in situations or relationships that are not good for you.

Forgiving Does Not Imply Forgetting

According to a 2015 study by Lichtenfield, et. al., they suggest that there are two types of forgiveness: decisional and emotional.

- **Decisional forgiveness** means you actively choose to let go of negative emotions such as anger and resentment. By doing so, you can leave these feelings in the past and move forward without being held back by their effects.
- **Emotional forgiveness** means you replace negative feelings towards the person who has

wronged you with positive emotions like sympathy, compassion, or empathy.

You are most likely familiar with the adage "Forgive and forget". Experts say that the chance of forgetting is higher when you "emotionally forgive" than when you "decisionally forgive" (Noreen & MacLeod, 2021).

But when you forgive someone, it does not necessarily mean that you forget what they have done, as it is not possible in every situation. Forgiving the offender can be challenging to do, after all. "Forgiving and forgetting" is a choice, and if you choose not to forget, you can still use the learnings from your experience to help you cope if you ever encounter similar toxic behaviors in the future.

The Personal Power of True Forgiveness

Understanding the deep meaning of forgiveness is one of the most important things that you can do on your path to becoming a better person. This process of change is about reclaiming your mental independence from the wrongs and offenses you encountered in the past. When you choose to forgive, you are letting go of the pain and anger that is still hanging over you. This lets you move on with a lighter heart and a new sense of purpose.

Myths and false beliefs can make it hard to see what forgiveness is really like, which can lead you astray or give you the wrong idea about how deep it goes. But once you get past these false beliefs, you will see the raw, life-changing power that real forgiveness has. It is not a sign of weakness or giving up; it is a sign of power, resilience, and a deep understanding of yourself.

When you truly forgive, you not only heal your heart, but you also set off a chain reaction that leads to better relationships and a clearer, more peaceful road through life. Realizing and using this transformative power can give you a new viewpoint and help you connect with yourself and the world around you more deeply.

6.3 JOURNEYING TOWARDS CLOSURE

Closure safeguards our hearts from painful memories, offering protection from the cold, difficult traumas of the past. It helps to heal emotional wounds and move forward in life. By working with your emotions, you can transform negative feelings into positive qualities like strength and wisdom. Seeking closure involves addressing the relationships and events that have impacted and changed you, so you can accept, heal, and grow from them. You must face your past and let go of any negative feelings associated with it. This will enable you to move forward with positivity and strength.

The process of closure is a way to settle conflicts with your interpersonal connections. It means not only realizing and accepting what happened, but also letting go of the memories of it. Moving on does not mean you have to forget or delete these reminders of the past. Instead, it is about carrying them with ease, free of the heavy chains of anger or longing, so they serve as lessons instead of burdens.

There are various ways to find peace and different people have unique paths that lead them there. Some people seek resolution in conflicts and crave explanations to soothe their minds, while others prefer to look inward and find solace in spiritual practices, self-reflection, or conversations with themselves. Regardless of the path you choose, you will ultimately be led to the same destination: a heart that is free from the distressing echoes of the past, ready to embrace the present and the future.

Understanding Acceptance

Acceptance is a deep idea that lies at the heart of closure. It is a subtle but powerful force that shapes the path of our mental healing. Acceptance isn't just giving up or recognizing what happened; it is an active process that involves deeply recognizing all the different experiences, feelings, and outcomes that have happened in your life.

To really understand acceptance, you need to know how it works on a deeper level. Accepting something doesn't mean you agree with or enjoy past hurts or losses. Instead, it is about understanding these events as they really were, without any denial or wishful thought getting in the way. It is about letting the range of feelings that come up with these memories, from anger to sadness, exist without giving in to the urge to hide them or change them.

Acceptance also makes it possible to really look inside yourself. By accepting events and feelings with an open heart, you can come to understand the roles you played, the lessons you taught or learned, and the scars you left behind. This deep awareness makes it easier for you to release the past and take control of your own healing journey.

In your journey to healing, every feeling and action affects and feeds into the big picture of mending. In order to move forward toward closure, you must first accept what happened in the past. Only then can you find the strength and understanding to do so.

The Many Avenues to Closure

The search for closure is deeply personal and has many aspects. It does not always look like grand gestures or dramatic confrontations, which is how most people think of it mainly because of the many movies and books that often romanticize these. But the real truth of closure is much more complex and personal. For many, peace is found during quiet moments of reflection.

There are as many different ways to find peace as there are people who want it. Some people find relief in writing in a notebook, where the ink captures and holds their tumultuous feelings, giving them a way to let go and a physical record of their journey. For others, the structured environment of therapy is a safe haven where they can talk about their past traumas with the caring eye of a trained expert, which helps them understand and heal. Many people have also found comfort in spiritual practices, which help them find their way through past hardships and into the tranquility of acceptance and peace.

Some hurts from your past can become less painful as time goes by, making them easier to deal with and finally letting go of. In the end, all of these different roads lead to the same place: a place where the past doesn't hold back the present, and your heart finds its rhythm again, free from the weight of what was. It is important to recognize and respect these different paths to peace, knowing that everyone is different and shaped by their own experiences, needs, and deepest thoughts. What works for one person may not work for another, so take some time to try and find what works best for you.

Letting Go of What Was

Letting go is often the most difficult part of coming to terms with something. While it may seem straightforward to describe, it is actually more complicated to carry out. It stands between the haunting sounds of the past and the promise of a free present. It is not enough to just physically move away from what was; we also have to find our way through the complex web of feelings, memories, and dreams that have wrapped themselves around our minds.

When you let go, you free your heart from the things of the past that are no longer important to you but still cast a shadow over the present. It is a choice that does not take away from or lessen the importance of past events, but rather acknowledges that their time and place belong somewhere else. There is no need to erase or paint over memories with this act. Instead, it is about changing how you relate to those memories so they become lessons instead of chains.

Also, getting free from the past is not a one-time thing; it is a process that never ends. Even though old attachments, dreams, and deep-seated emotional ties may try to pull you back, you can cut them off if you want to. This way, they won't be able to cloud your vision or stop you from moving forward. When you truly let go, you give yourself the freedom to fully experience the present, to breathe in the now without the weight of what was, and to make a way forward with hope, clarity, and new energy.

The Liberating Embrace of Closure

The act of seeking and embracing closure is nothing short of granting yourself a profound form of self-liberation. It involves decisively shedding past burdens, casting off lingering emotions, and claiming the space to breathe without the shackles of uncertainty. The path, though winding and fraught with challenges, is illuminated by the promise of tranquility and understanding that awaits at its end.

Every step towards closure, while occasionally steeped in moments of introspection and nostalgia, is a movement towards a clearer horizon where the past does not dictate the contours of the present. It is about understanding and coming to terms with events and emotions, not as chains that bind, but as chapters of a narrative that has shaped us. Each chapter, while significant, doesn't have to overshadow the unfolding story.

Ultimately, the embrace of closure is not just about ending a chapter or turning a page; it is about allowing yourself the grace and space to start a new narrative. A narrative where lessons from the past provide the wisdom for the present and the hope for the future. The journey, with all its complexities, is an affirmation of the resilience of the human spirit, proving that peace is attainable, even in the aftermath of difficult times.

6.4 THE RELEASE OF ANGER AND BITTERNESS

Resentment is like a shadow that follows you around, slowly dimming the light of your inner joy. It is often quiet but deeply felt. At first, it seems like a harmless emotion—a brief sting from a past grudge or an imagined slight. But if you do not deal with it, it burrows deep into your mind and becomes a heavy, constant companion that affects how you act, make choices, and feel.

As time goes on, it becomes clearer how sneaky anger can be. It stops staying in your emotions and starts showing up in real ways, like changing how you act, making your relationships harder, and even affecting your health. As a result, you often do not notice how it affects your daily life until they are so ingrained that you cannot live without them.

There are many steps to take to understand anger. It is about figuring out where it came from, how it affects you deeply, and how much it can change your world. To truly break free from its grip, the first and most important thing is to recognize its presence and the huge impact it has on your overall health.

Anger's Toll on Well-being

Like a pot slowly cooking, anger can significantly affect many parts of your life if you don't do anything about it. That feeling is not just a passing feeling; it is a strong force that can change the way how your body, relationships, and mind works. If you do not deal with this overpowering emotion, it can spill over over time and leave marks in places you might not instantly connect with its presence.

Holding on to anger can have serious long-term effects on your health. Anger causes your adrenaline to keep pumping, which can raise your blood pressure and make you more likely to develop anxiety disorders. In the long run, these physiological stresses can turn into more serious illnesses, like heart disease or depression. This shows how closely our mental and physical health are connected.

When uncontrolled, your anger not only hurts you personally but also significantly impacts your relationships with others, including family, romantic partners, and friends. It impairs your ability to make sound decisions, communicate effectively, and empathize with others. Viewing the world through a lens of anger makes it challenging for you to engage, connect, and foster healthy relationships, and sometimes repairing the damage can seem impossible to fix.

To sum up, understanding anger means recognizing the various effects it can have. It is not just a fleeting emotion; it is a powerful force that can affect your health, relationships, and overall perspective on life. I cannot stress enough how important it is to learn to handle it and eventually let it go.

The Path to Understanding Pain

We often have to go through the valleys of our own pain. On this path, you have to be honest with yourself and go deep into the hurts you want to avoid. To truly understand your pain, where it comes from, and how it affects your mind on a deep level is a delicate and sometimes frightening journey.

There is more to it than just drowning in sadness or dwelling on old grudges. Instead, it is about giving yourself time and room to recognize the hurt. To be resilient, you may often push your feelings to the side. This is about giving those feelings a voice. Every emotion, every hurt, and every tear you shed is a thread in your life fabric. When you recognize and talk about these feelings, you start a healing process that is important for real recovery.

This self-reflection is definitely hard, but it is a key part of turning pain into knowledge. When you face your deepest hurts, try to understand where they came from and figure out what lessons they can teach you. You can gain insights that shape how you connect, make decisions, and act in the future. Even though the road may have moments when you feel weak, it will eventually lead to a clearing—a spot where anger fades, and growth and clarity take its place.

To really understand pain, it is not so much about getting there as it is about walking the path itself. Transformation is what changes us from victims of past hurts to creators of our own healing and well-being.

Choosing Compassion Over Bitterness

The moment when you choose the soft embrace of kindness over the sharp edges of bitterness is a moment of deep change. This important decision may seem small, but it can have a huge effect on your path to healing and health. Being compassionate means giving the other person a moment of peace and helping to heal scars that have been open for too long.

It is important to remember that kindness goes in two important directions: toward yourself and toward those who may have caused you pain. Being compassionate toward yourself means recognizing how strong you are to get through pain and how brave you are to choose healing over holding on to grudges. When you do this, you show yourself love, accept your worth, and allow yourself to heal at your own pace.

Being compassionate with people who have hurt you does not mean giving them a clean start or downplaying the gravity of what they did. Instead, you have to make a choice inside yourself to break free from the chains of constant anger. It is about realizing that holding on to anger can hurt you more than the person who hurt you. When you show compassion, you are basically choosing a path of empathy, a path that helps you understand human flaws and the complicated way emotions affect how we deal with each other.

Basically, choosing kindness over anger is the same thing as choosing light over darkness. You have to choose to find inner peace, care for your mind, and create a space where healing can really take hold. By making this choice, you show that you are committed to your health and happiness, and you begin a path that will be full of growth, understanding, and peace.

Embracing the Future with Open Arms

Letting go of anger and hatred leads to a new beginning—that feeling of having the weight lifted off your shoulders, letting your heart beat more freely, free from the chains of past hurts and guilt. This deep release not only cleans the mental palette but it also refreshes the spirit and gives you a new way to see the world.

This new point of view opens up a world of opportunities with every step forward. It makes it easier to build stronger, more important relationships with other people based on trust and understanding. Being free of the haze of old grudges means that you can fully enjoy the present, savoring every moment, interaction, and feeling with a fresh sense of wonder.

This change in emotions creates an atmosphere where real happiness can grow. It is a happiness that comes from the inside, not from outside approval. It is a satisfaction that comes from knowing you have faced your inner demons, fought them, and won. When you are in this state of inner harmony, you value life's simple pleasures more and are more thankful for the complicated situations that shape you.

Letting go and letting out those feelings that have been building up is like starting a new part of your life story. In this part, the past, with its lessons and scars, is just a background. The future, with its endless possibilities, becomes the main focus, and you can look forward to it, full of hope, promise, and endless opportunities.

6.5 CRAFTING A LIFE OF PEACE AND PURPOSE

.People often go through big changes when they are facing many problems in life. Post-traumatic growth is the name for this life-changing event that shows how the human spirit can rise and rebuild. People often do not just go back to how they were before they went through a hard time; they often come out of it stronger, smarter, and more resilient. Instead of trying to erase the scars of the past, this evolution is more about turning them into badges of honor that show off the fights won and the lessons learned.

This growth is what makes it so powerful. When you go through hard times, you will discover how strong, how persistent and how determined you really are. You will learn just how much you can handle and achieve through these challenging experiences.

To fully accept post-traumatic growth means to be aware of the pain and problems you have been through and to use them to grow as a person. Make the choice not to let the problems define you; instead use them as stepping stones to build a better, more educated future.

Human Resilience: Bouncing Back Stronger

You have the ability to handle life's challenges effectively through persistence. By being resilient, you can adapt to and recover from difficult situations. People have shown throughout history that they can not only get through hard times, but also come out of them with more energy, wisdom, and a greater love for life. You can be one of those people.

Healing from these experiences does not always mean returning to a previous state. Instead, it often leads to a greater understanding and perspective. Challenges can drive you on a life-changing journey, demonstrating your strength and determination. They show that you can not only survive but also grow, using past experiences to evolve and become more wise.

Realizing that resilience is not just about the battles won or the problems solved is a key part of this natural power. This is a celebration of human potential and a statement that we can turn pain into purpose, problems into chances, and setbacks into stepping stones. From this point of view, resilience is not just a way to stay alive; it is also a way to find our way forward with meaning and newfound hope.

Discovering Meaning Amidst Chaos

Life can be full of unexpected challenges that can make things seem chaotic and confusing. However, these challenges can also lead to self-reflection and deep thinking. By navigating through these difficulties, you can connect with your inner self and gain a deeper understanding of life. Overcoming adversity can lead to insights that can bring lasting meaning and happiness.

Remember, peace of mind doesn't require peace and quiet. *(Vincenty, 2022)*. Even with all the chaos surrounding you, whether it be the people or the noise of daily life, you can close your eyes and find the space of calmness within you. Practice visualization and find your happy place and what gives your life meaning. It is okay if it takes you a while to find this, but the more you do it, the easier it will be for you to eventually find this.

"Making meaning out of what happened to you is seeing the possibilities that are now open to you as a direct result of your suffering" (*Enright and North, 1998*) is one way to look at it. It is possible that despite your experiences, the love you are capable of giving can still make a difference in other people's lives in the future with time and support. This may pave the way for something else that could never have occurred otherwise. Though it may feel overwhelming, the suffering and chaos you have gone through are not permanent, even if your loss is. The meaning of life might just be to find purpose in all that it offers and for you to live accordingly.

CRAFTING A LIFE ALIGNED WITH TRUE VALUES

It can be very hard to find and stick to your core ideals when there are many outside expectations and social pressures. You can see more clearly what really speaks to your soul, though, when you look inside yourself and think about the things you have been through. This clarity becomes the compass that will help you make decisions that are more in line with your core views and goals in life.

Every choice made, every friendship cared for, and every project started will show a more true reflection of yourself. This harmonious alignment with your values does more than just make it easier to make choices; it also gives you a feeling of inner peace and cohesion. This balance, which comes from living a life that is in line with your true beliefs, not only improves your health but also makes daily things more satisfying and joyful. When things are in balance, happiness is not fleeting. There is a lasting contentment that comes from knowing that key ideals are shaping your life.

Celebrating Moments of Joy and Serenity

Life is a set of moments, each with its own beauty and meaning, when seen through the lens of clarity and self-reflection. Some moments, like the soft warmth of the morning sun or an unplanned laugh with a close friend, are so beautiful because they are so simple. Others stand out because they make you feel strong feelings, like the pride that comes with a job well done. All of these events, big and small, add up to make up the colorful landscape of your life.

When you recognize and fully experience these moments, you connect with a deeper source of peace and calm, which lets your soul enjoy the peace that life provides. Every beat of the heart, every breath, and every little detail in between are reasons to celebrate and a reminder of how joyful life is.

Making a life full of peace and meaning is not about getting to a clear endpoint. Be grateful for everything that happens and also for what does *not* happen. Practice acceptance of the things that are out of your control, even though it can be challenging. Just like other things that you practice, when you keep doing it, it will eventually become easier. Learn from the lessons along the way, and keep growing. Embracing this always-changing path with interest, gratitude, and hope will open the door to a life full of happiness, meaning, and endless wonder.

* * *

Having taken the important strides of forgiveness and closure, we will next address overcoming codependency, another aspect of our healing journey in the next chapter.

CHAPTER 7: OVERCOMING CODEPENDENCY

Melissa had an alarming realization as she thought about her past relationships. In her sincere efforts to be the perfect partner, she had focused so much on meeting her partner's every whim and need that she had forgotten about her own wants, needs, and mental health, like disregarded scribbled notes in the margins of a book. The memories of the past came back to her with a single, haunting chant that seemed to describe all of her relationships: codependency.

It was not just about giving up things or compromising, which are normal things to talk about in a serious relationship. There was something more sneaky going on here. Her identity became so mixed up with her partner's that she couldn't tell the difference between them. The truth was both harsh and disturbing.

Starting out, this chapter will help you understand the complex web of codependency by looking into its causes, how it shows up in real life, and most importantly, the ways in which you can regain your sense of self-worth, independence, and identity.

7.1 SIGNS AND SYMPTOMS OF CODEPENDENCY

Starting on the path to healing is a lot like setting sail on waters you have never been on before. Having been able to sail my own way myself, I can only help guide you. Now you must take reigns and navigate this. It is important to find the small winds and currents that may have tossed you off course before you can guide the ship back to safety. These subtleties, which are often hard to notice at first glance, have a big impact on how you feel.

Codependency stands out as one of these mysterious forces like a siren's song that pulls at the very core of your relationship compass in a powerful way. It leads you to prioritize someone else's identity, needs, and wants over your own, creating patterns of behavior that are hard to break.

So, if you want to change your life for the better and have healthy relationships, the first thing you need to do is really pay attention to these signs of codependency. Only then can you find a path that will make you happy and allow you to stay true to who you are.

1. Excessive reliance on others for validation: You have an overriding need for approval and an aversion to rejection, often causing you to go to great lengths to avoid displeasing others.
2. Sacrificing your own needs: You consistently put others' needs and desires above your own, even at the cost of your well-being.
3. Low self-esteem: You have a persistent negative self-image, feelings of inadequacy, and doubts about your worth or value.
4. Boundary issues: You have difficulty placing interpersonal limits, leading to blurred personal boundaries.
5. Fear of abandonment: You have a heightened fear of being left alone or rejected, leading to tolerating maltreatment or staying in unhealthy situations.
6. Denial: You ignore or downplay personal feelings and needs or the problems within a relationship, and you invest energy in "rescuing" or "fixing" others.

7.2 ROOT CAUSES OF CODEPENDENCY

A lot of times, the pattern of codependency starts to form when you are still very young. Initially, the individual threads may not seem harmful on their own, but over time, they weave together to create a complex and binding cloth that significantly impacts how you interact with others.

This pattern is influenced by various factors and inspirations, which take root in your formative years. These influences can stem from your family environments, early childhood memories, or even your first dates. As they grow in the background, they establish habits and behaviors that may seem normal or necessary at the time.

Some habits and tendencies become so ingrained that they become part of your relationship DNA over time. It is important to look back at these causes in order to fully understand the scope and depth of codependency. This will put light on the shadows of our past that still affect our present.

1. Dysfunctional family dynamics: Growing up in environments where emotions were discounted or not expressed, where there was addiction, or where emotional needs are not met, can lay the groundwork for codependent behaviors in adulthood.
2. Past trauma or abuse: Experiencing emotional, physical, or sexual abuse can lead to a distorted sense of self-worth and an excessive need for external validation.
3. Societal and cultural influences: Societal norms that stress selflessness or care for others at the expense of yourself can sometimes exacerbate tendencies towards codependency.

7.3 BREAKING THE CHAINS: BUILDING SELF-RELIANCE

Getting through the maze of codependency is without a doubt hard and needs a determined and caring approach. To break free from its hold, you cannot just make quick fixes or surface changes. Instead, you have to go on a journey that changes you at the core, leading to self-awareness, strength, and personal growth. It can feel like a huge step forward every time, especially when it seems like ghosts from the past are trying to pull you back into old habits.

A gentle reminder to those who see a loved one deal with codependency: compassion is very important. The person's emotional ups and downs may sometimes cause them to respond or defend themselves in ways they did not expect. Being more understanding with others by realizing that their actions are not personal attacks but signs of greater problems can help people get along better with each other.

There are, in fact, a lot of different ways to deal with the problems that codependency causes. Still, it is important to remember that these methods may look easy on paper, but they require patience, persistence, and self-forgiveness to use in real life. There are obstacles on the path to healing, but they are not impossible. Every effort, no matter how small, shows how strong the human spirit is and how much people want to improve themselves.

- Developing self-awareness: Recognizing and acknowledging codependent patterns is the first step towards change.
- Setting healthy boundaries: Understand your limits and communicate them clearly in relationships.
- Seeking professional help: Therapy can offer insights into the origins of codependent behaviors and provide coping strategies.
- Building self-esteem: Engage in activities that foster a sense of achievement, set personal goals, and practice self-compassion and self-care.
- Cultivating independence: Take time to be alone, understand your personal desires, and make decisions independently to allow yourself to build a sense of self-reliance.

7.4 THE JOURNEY AHEAD

Coming out of codependency is like seeing the first light of day after a long night. With the weight of past actions and habits starting to drop, a world full of opportunities for relationships built on trust, understanding, and shared accountability lies ahead. Even if the path is filled with obstacles, it ultimately becomes a demonstration of your fortitude, dedication, and will to develop sincere relationships that uplift the spirit.

Promises of a better future await you as you break free from codependency. The absence of outdated norms is just one aspect of this new vista. Other aspects that shine through include self-respect, autonomy, and purpose. Your relationships have the capacity to develop into partnerships where both sides prosper and learn from one another, free from imbalance and sacrifice.

However, this transformation marks a fresh beginning rather than merely an end. It is a place to start from where the knowledge gained from the past serves as a roadmap for the future. Having broken the bonds of codependency, the future presents a clean slate. It is a chance to comprehend and lay the fundamental groundwork for wholesome relationships, guaranteeing that the path ahead is not only clear of the chains of the past but also full of harmony, happiness, and common goals.

CHAPTER 8: MOVING FORWARD WITH HEALTHY RELATIONSHIPS

After ending a toxic relationship, Melissa felt hesitant to pursue new romantic connections. She feared that she would repeat the same patterns of behavior that led to her previous relationship's toxicity. Fortunately, with the right tools and resources, she was finally able to heal and move forward.

In this final chapter, we will explore the possibility of moving forward with healthy relationships after a toxic one. We will explore practical tips and insights on how to build healthy connections with others. Whether you are looking to cultivate new relationships or deepen existing ones, you will have the tools and guidelines on how to approach relationships with intention and mindfulness and establish healthy patterns of communication and behavior.

You are a survivor and you *can* break free from the cycle of toxic relationships, and you deserve and *can* build fulfilling, healthy relationships from this point forward.

8.1 HEALTHY RELATIONSHIP ESSENTIALS

In a healthy relationship, respect, trust, and open communication are essential things that should exist between two people. Each one should be willing to put effort into the relationship and be willing to compromise. And I must say this as a reminder: If or when the relationship ends, each one should let the other person be free and move on.

Respect: Being Valued and Heard

Respect for one another is important in any healthy relationship. It is not just about acknowledging or tolerating each other—it is about truly understanding each other's thoughts, feelings, and opinions. When you both respect each other at this level, you guarantee that you are deeply present in your connection.

Living and working in a respectful environment means seeing and affirming each other's true selves. When you feel validated, it creates a caring atmosphere where you can talk openly, celebrate differences, and embrace vulnerabilities. Each of you feels valued, heard, and understood in this environment.

This foundation of respect opens the door to a deeper emotional connection. Even in disagreements, you should rely on respectful and thoughtful treatment from each other. Each one should respect each other's independence and be able to make and share decisions without fear of consequences. At the same time, each one should be able to find ways to meet each other's needs and boundaries in ways that you both feel comfortable with. The constant presence of respect keeps your relationship harmonious, caring, and deeply rooted.

<u>Trust: The Confidence that Bonds</u>

Trust becomes the deep, quiet force that makes real relationships possible. You cannot just get it or give it to someone without thinking about it first; it is not something you can take for granted. It takes time and actions that you can count on. When you keep your word and follow through on your promises, you plant the seeds of trust. Over time, those seeds grow and take root in the rich soil of mutual respect and understanding.

These roots grow and connect with shared memories, experiences, and moments, building a base that cannot be shaken by even life's worst storms. As trust grows stronger, it gives the relationship a safe place to start from which it can stretch, grow, and hit new heights.

The beautiful thing about trust is that it is both fragile and strong at the same time. Even though it can handle many problems when it is strong, it needs kindness, care, and constant nurturing. Recognizing how important trust is in a relationship is essential because it takes a lot of work to rebuild trust once it has been broken. Are you on the same

CHAPTER 8: MOVING FORWARD WITH HEALTHY RELA... | 123

page with this thought? When each one makes the effort to protect and nourish it, it becomes the guiding light that leads you to lasting closeness and understanding with each other.

When someone feels passionate about you, like in romantic relationships in particular, it is not enough to make big moves or promises and expect those things to earn your trust. Trust is built on everyday actions that each one does over and over again, like keeping small promises, being reliable in both everyday and difficult situations, and having honest conversations that reveal each one's true self. In any relationship, choosing to be there for each other with all of your heart is what builds trust.

Trust is not something that stays the same regardless of time or place. It becomes like an ongoing project for each person. Key turning points happen when you share your deepest fears or goals and are met with understanding and compassion from the other person. When you talk to each other in private, without judging each other and with mutual respect, trust grows and solidifies, becoming the rock-solid base of your relationship.

Hand-in-hand with trust is honesty. Being honest, open, and transparent with your partner is more than just a trait; it is a choice. When people are this honest, it provides a safe space where everyone feels comfortable talking about their thoughts, feelings, and goals, knowing that others will understand and care.

But this commitment to telling the truth is not just about big or important reveals; it is also in the little things that happen every day, in the way you talk to each other. One of the best things about being so open is that it keeps misunderstandings from happening. Neglected misunderstandings can often grow into bigger problems that hurt the relationship. Honesty, on the other hand, can help you avoid these problems, keeping the bond strong and clear.

When both of you have this trust, it helps ensure that no matter what problems come up in life, you are on the same page and can move forward together.

Good Communication: The Bridge to Understanding

Good communication is essential in relationships. It is more than simply a verbal conversation; it becomes the link that builds a strong tie with one another and helps overcome misunderstandings. It allows you to share who you are and what you need from the people around you. Open communication turns obstacles into learning experiences, enhances happy moments, and builds a deeper level of intimacy that goes beyond superficial relationships. With sentiments acknowledged, worries handled, and goals communicated, such open lines of communication ensure a mutual understanding.

In addition to the responsibilities of a relationship, there are joyful moments of laughter, private jokes, and cherished memories that keep the bond strong and vibrant. With this foundation, relationships become more than agreements; they become strong bonds that support and encourage each other, creating meaningful and memorable experiences.

Here are a few helpful guidelines to keep in mind:

- **Speaking:** Be clear and open about your feelings; if something is unclear, ask for clarification. Use "I statements" to avoid sounding accusatory, for example: "I feel that..."). Be honest, even if it might be uncomfortable. Apologize when you are wrong, and balance negative feedback with positive remarks. For any important conversations, it is always better to have them in person rather than over text or online, and to talk when you are calm or at least have had some time to cool down if you had a disagreement.
- **Listening:** Focus on the speaker without distractions. Listen to understand, not just to respond. Let them finish before you speak, and use acknowledging phrases like "interesting" to show you're engaged. If something is unclear, ask questions to avoid misunderstandings. If you need time to respond, let them know. Be prepared to hear things you might not like and take time to reflect before replying.
- **Body Language:** Maintain eye contact, face the person, and give your full attention, leaning in as they speak to show you're engaged.

8.2 NURTURING RELATIONSHIP BONDS

Every connection we have, even the ones that end in heartbreak, teaches us something very important. These interactions, which include happy times, hard times, and sometimes painful endings, leave lessons that will never go away. The beauty of these lessons is not just their depth, but also how they can change you. We learn more about relationships and our place in them with each experience, whether it's the soft touch of love or the pain of betrayal.

Most of the time, the scars are from situations that pushed us to our limits. But they do more than just remind us of pain; they stand as quiet reminders to make us more careful in the future. They help us remember when we crossed lines, when we broke trust, and when we made deals that might have cost us our peace. However, mixed in with these sobering memories are the sweet times we have had with love, which remind us of the depths of connection and happiness we can feel.

With these echoes from the past, we can better understand how to manage the future. This storehouse of information, which includes both good and bad things, guides us away from making the same mistakes again and toward deeper, more meaningful connections. In the end, all of the problems we have had in the past with other people have taught us how to make the future full of understanding, growth, and of real connections.

Rebuilding Trust After Betrayal

As much as we try our best to keep the trust within our relationship, what if that trust is broken? Even though broken trust can be very painful, it does not always mean the end of the relationship. Instead, you can view it as a challenge that will test how strong and resilient your relationship bond is. The person who broke the trust has a lot of responsibility to get through this rough patch. For that person, the first step is to honestly admit that you did something wrong without making any excuses. After that, a genuine desire to make things right and a clear effort to stop the bad behavior from happening again are very important.

In the same way, or even more so, the road is hard for the other person who was betrayed. It is important to let them say how much they hurt and how disappointed they are, and to set clear limits for the future. But the real challenge is in the act of forgiving in the end. Making the choice to heal and move on with a positive outlook on the future is what this means, not forgetting or lessening the effects of the betrayal.

As both of you start to rebuild your lives together, you will need to be patient and committed to each other. Both of you must work to understand, re-learn, and strengthen the things that hold your relationship together. There may be times when you question yourself, and memories of the breach of trust may sometimes make the present seem less clear. However, if you keep at it, the fog can lift and show you a relationship that is even stronger after a big storm.

Every relationship has its ups and downs, but at their core, they are still beautiful and complex, and need care and attention. Remember that trust, which is very fragile, is what holds this relationship together. Knowing how fragile the relationship is and making a promise to keep it in good shape are the only ways to make sure it stays strong even when things go wrong.

Navigating through Disagreement

There will be rough patches in every relationship, no matter how good it is. It is what happens when you mix two different worlds, each with its own ideals, beliefs, and expectations. But the real test of a relationship is not whether or not there are differences; it is how well they are handled with maturity and grace. To get through these rare storms, you need to be patient, understanding, and respectful of each other.

Even though disagreements are unavoidable, they can be used to grow and understand each other better. The key is to use helpful ways to solve disagreements. Avoiding contempt, looking for "repair attempts" when there are misunderstandings, and encouraging open communication are all important ways to keep disagreements from turning into rifts. It is not enough to just settle disagreements; you need to find common meaning in them too. Recognizing shared goals, highlighting shared aspirations, and discovering a middle ground can turn these times of disagreement into turning points that improve relationships. Getting through each problem shows how strong the relationship is, making the base it stands on even stronger.

You need to communicate effectively with more than just words. Use body language, attentive listening, and sincere responses. Picking up on the little things matters, that is, the thoughts and wishes that are not said. By working on these skills, you are not "just talking"; you connect and create a story in which each person contributes in their own unique way to a shared story of love, understanding, and mutual respect.

Equality: The Balance of Roles

Equality becomes the beat that keeps each person in a relationship in sync with each other. There is more to true equality than just sharing roles and responsibilities. It is the belief that everyone, no matter how different they are, deserves to stand on equal ground and have their opinions, hopes, and feelings heard. There is more to this than just being fair; it shows how much respect and love each of you has for each other.

When each person in a relationship works hard to keep this balance, it is a beautiful way to show respect for each other. Each partner not only listens, but also truly values the other person's unique needs, goals, and limits. This kind of setting encourages open communication, mutual understanding, and agreement.

Equality helps people connect and trust each other more. It is easier for each person in the relationship to feel safe and respected when they both feel heard and recognized. The result is a relationship where both people can find comfort in knowing they have an equal stake in their shared journey, no matter what life throws at them. They can live through life with grace, understanding, and real connection.

From Hope to Embracing Future Possibilities

There are many opportunities to change and improve your relationships in the future that lies ahead of you. Each new day presents fresh chances to form meaningful connections. Even though your past affects these new interactions, they aren't limited or dictated by old habits. Instead, they enable you to strive to build relationships based on love, understanding, and respect.

Transitioning from hope to reality takes time and patience, along with ongoing effort and dedication in relationships. Introspection, involving understanding your beliefs, goals, and desires, is important in creating this healthy relationship blueprint. It is about appreciating and accepting yourself and establishing expectations and boundaries for mutual respect in a relationship.

Implementing the relationship blueprint is key, as relationships evolve over time. Past experiences, which include both good and bad times, as well as lessons learned, affect how you see and understand your present relationships. They help you navigate which roads are worth taking and which ones you should avoid. The beautiful thing about the future, though, is that it is always changing and can bring new routes and stories. Every new person you meet and every interaction you have is a blank slate ready to be filled with respect, understanding, and mutually fulfilling relationships.

As you hold on to the lessons you learned yesterday, you can approach the future with self-awareness, intentional actions, and commitment to mutual growth. With a hopeful and purposeful mindset, you can develop satisfying and lasting relationships with a deep understanding and connection to enrich your life more than before.

8.3 BUILDING A DEEPER CONNECTION

Turning toward each other is an important part of a healthy connection. This action shows more than just being close physically. When you really tune into the other person and pick up on the unspoken emotions, mood changes, and wants, that's what attentiveness is all about. This action says a lot about how close you are, whether it is through a quiet talk, a soft touch, or just the warm hug of understanding silence.

The simple act of turning to another person becomes even more important when you feel weak or unsure. These small moments, which might not seem important at first, are great chances to strengthen the bond. When you each choose to be present in these situations, both mentally and physically, you build trust and mutual respect one brick at a time.

These small acts of involvement and connection add up over time, building a pool of goodwill and understanding. This collection becomes the relationship's backbone. It ensures that even when life brings problems, the bond stays strong because it is based on many intentional times of connection and support.

Separate Identities: The Essence of Individual Growth

People whose lives come together often share memories and experiences; however, the real beauty of these connections emerges when each person maintains their uniqueness. Even in an intimate space, personal pursuits, passions, and dreams can flourish. This uniqueness does not make the connection less strong; instead, it deepens it by adding new perspectives and opportunities for growth.

Taking care of each one's separate identities does more than just maintain individuality; it also helps the relationship grow. When each one is involved in their own hobbies and activities, they are able to bring back new experiences to share. It helps bring something fresh. You wouldn't want anything that's stale after all, would you? This keeps the talks going and the relationship alive. At the same time, celebrate, respect, and enjoy each other's unique interests to show your trust and admiration for each other.

Staying true to yourself keeps the relationship healthy and alive. It shows that real love is not about losing yourself; it is about joining together as two whole people, with each person adding something special to the relationship. This makes sure that the relationship bond is both satisfying and peaceful.

The Art of Compromise

It is normal and expected for people to have different thoughts and opinions. After all, everyone sees the world through their own unique lens, which is made up of their own experiences, views, and values. Still, these differences are a beautiful chance for growth, learning, and getting closer to each other. It is not that there are no disagreements in a relationship; it is that each person can handle them with ease and find a happy medium.

Accepting is more than just recognizing these differences; it is a way of showing that you value and honor them. It means you are ready to put yourself in the other person's shoes and see things from their point of view, even if only for a short time. This small but meaningful action shows the other person that you not only understand and value their feelings, goals, and points of view, but also respect them.

When two people are open to each other's ideas and willing to let each other influence them, they make decisions or choices together. Every decision or choice, no matter how big or small, is a combination of each person's ideas, making sure that the end result fits both of their wants and needs. This collaborative decision-making process not only produces results but also strengthens the bond between the two people by fostering mutual respect and understanding.

A feeling of balance and fairness naturally grows in this kind of situation. Over time, mutual respect and the willingness to compromise strengthen the relationship's base, making it stronger in the face of problems. It is based on shared values and love for each other.

Keeping the Flame Alive

In romantic relationships, all of our daily tasks and responsibilities can make it hard to see the little things that make a relationship truly special. The small acts, shared smiles, and fleeting moments that sparked the fire in the first place can slowly fade into the background as life moves faster and faster. But it's these little things, these powerful sparks, that keep a relationship going and make it shine better even when things go wrong.

Taking a moment to think about your partner and tell them you admire them goes beyond just saying "thank you." It is a sign of the bond, the journey you have been on together, and the treasures you have found along the way. Whether it is a sincere compliment on a partner's strengths, a thank-you for their unwavering support, or just a note of appreciation for the beauty in their quirks and idiosyncrasies, these statements bring new life and warmth to the relationship.

These displays of respect aren't just nice to do; they are also important for the relationship because they strengthen it. They are gentle reminders of all the reasons two people decided to go through life together. Partners can create a positive environment where they both feel seen, loved, and valued by actively showing admiration.

A good, helpful guideline to follow is the Magic Five Hours by psychologist John Gottman *(Gottman, 1999)*:

1. **Parting:** before saying goodbyes in the morning, find out one thing which is happening in your partner's life that day;
2. **Reunions:** stress-reducing conversations at the end of each workday;
3. **Admiration and appreciation:** find some way every day to communicate genuine affection and appreciation towards your spouse;
4. **Affection:** kiss, hold, grab and touch each other when together;
5. **Weekly dates:** could be a relaxing low-pressure way to stay connected. Ask each other questions [to update your love-maps] and turn towards each other. Talking out a marital issue or working through an argument can also be done here.

Keeping the respect flame alive is a lot like taking care of a fragile but strong plant. The relationship grows stronger with regular care, like showing genuine appreciation and recognition. It turns into a bond of mutual respect, deep affection, and lasting love.

8.4 THE IMPACT OF HEALTHY RELATIONSHIPS

Not only are good relationships important for your happiness, but they are also important for your overall health and well-being. Research highlights that strong social connections help people live longer, manage stress better, adopt healthier habits, and even have a stronger immune system. In fact, a 2010 study by Holt-Lundstad, Smith, and Layton found that people in long-term healthy relationships are 50% less likely to die prematurely than those without such connections, which in terms of life expectancy, those without them are as unhealthy as smoking! (Brickel, 2024).

Humans—you and I—are inherently social beings, and the quality of our relationships impacts our mental, emotional, and physical health. When we lack these connections, it goes beyond just living a lonely life; we suffer mentally and physically, according to the public health study by the CDC (Centers for Disease Control and Prevention) called the Adverse Childhood Experiences (ACE) study.

However, there is hope. A healthy relationship requires attunement—when people genuinely listen to and support each other, they foster a sense of safety and security. These connections help mitigate stress and anxiety, promoting better overall health.

Even if you have struggled with poor, toxic relationships in the past, it is never too late to build healthy ones. Therapy can be a significant space for learning how to form secure connections as it will help you learn that relationships can indeed be safe, supportive, and life-enhancing, and it is where you can work on the essentials of respect, trust, and open communication.

As an additional resource (if you haven't already), you can also read one of my other books, *5 Keys to Building Lifelong Healthy Relationships: Overcoming Trust Concerns, Setting Boundaries, Handling Conflict Positively for a Strong, Committed Partnership in Happiness and Love.*

Learning how to open up to others and form healthy relationships takes time, but it is definitely possible. You can do it and you should be proud of yourself for taking the steps for your happiness, health, and well-being.

A BEACON OF HOPE FOR HEALING AND GROWTH

Your experience matters. If you found solace, strength, or invaluable insights within the pages of this book, I invite you to share your thoughts.

If this book has helped shine the light on your pathway to recovery, rebuilding self-esteem, and establishing healthy boundaries, your review can resonate with others seeking similar paths. Your words have the power to inspire and reassure someone who may be navigating the challenges of toxic relationships.

By leaving a review on Amazon and/or Goodreads even with just a couple of lines, you become a part of a community fostering healing and growth. Your honest feedback can make a difference, offering encouragement to those taking steps on their own transformative journeys.

Thank you for being a part of this collective effort to support and uplift others. Your insights could be the beacon of hope someone needs.

CONCLUSION

In this book, we have looked at many different aspects of interactions. We have talked about the pros and cons of interpersonal connections, from spotting the signs of unhealthy relationships to understanding how important it is to forgive and move on. In addition, we have talked about how complicated codependency is and how to build good relationships.

The main thing I want you to remember from everything here is this: you are incredibly strong and resilient. This toughness not only helps you get over the problems in past relationships, but it also sets you up for future relationships based on shared growth, understanding, and respect. Take a look at Melissa's story, who went from having a hard past to having a bright future. She represents the promise that each reader has.

As we come to an end, it is important to keep in mind that growth and healing happen all the time. Use the ideas in this book to improve the way you communicate with other people every day. Focus on being kind to yourself, find people or groups that can help you when you need it, do self-care habits that work for you, be honest with the people around you, and stay open to new and good experiences.

Thank you for considering writing a review if this book spoke to you or helped you. Your feedback is very helpful, not just for me but also for other people who are trying to understand and improve the way their relationships work. It can be hard to understand relationships, but if we have the right tools and attitude, we can all make and keep ties that are meaningful and enriching. Don't forget to use what you've learned, and think about giving it to people who could use it.

FREE GIFT #2 FOR MY READERS

Just for you! As a thank you for being my valued reader, you can get this free ebook on 9 Guided Meditations to Deepen Your Intimacy and Communication in Your Relationship.

Visit ebook.arianeturpin.com/9meditations or scan the above QR code to access it.

ABOUT THE AUTHOR

Ariane S. Turpin writes about love, relationships, and family. She has won a Literary Titan Gold Book Award for her book, *5 Keys to Building Lifelong Healthy Relationships*.

Her personal experiences of love and heartbreak from her long-term relationships and pseudo-relationships, before marrying the love of her life in her 30s, as well as the wealth of learnings she has accumulated over the years are what inspired her to write her books. Her hope is that her books will help you be the best person you can be, and you can be with the best person for you.

She is an advocate for diversity, equity, and inclusion, and wants readers from various backgrounds to be able to relate to her books and find inspiration. When she's not writing, she loves to explore the outdoors and workout.

Visit Ariane's website to find out more about her upcoming books at www.arianeturpin.com .

facebook.com/arianeturpinauthor
x.com/arianeturpincom
instagram.com/arianeturpinauthor
tiktok.com/@arianeturpinauthor

ALSO BY ARIANE S. TURPIN

*5 Keys to Building Lifelong Healthy Relationships:
Overcoming Trust Concerns, Setting Boundaries,
Handling Conflict Positively for a Strong, Committed
Partnership in Happiness and Love*

Discover practical, proven strategies for creating and maintaining a loving, healthy partnership. Navigate better the inevitable challenges that arise in any relationship, even if you think everything is already common sense. Whether you're single and looking for love, or already in a relationship and seeking to improve it, create a life-changing partnership that lasts a lifetime from today!

Available on Amazon in Kindle edition, Paperback, Hardcover, and Audible audiobook.

https://www.amazon.com/author/arianeturpin

*The Self-Love Path: How to Embrace Self-Compassion
and Kindness to Yourself and Achieve Your Goals*

Unlock the incredible power of self-love while pursuing your goals. Take the first step towards an empowered life while you embrace your unique journey, celebrate your successes, and cultivate a deep sense of kindness and compassion towards yourself, even if you've struggled with self-doubt and setbacks in the past.

Available on Amazon in Kindle edition, Paperback, and Hardcover.

https://www.amazon.com/author/arianeturpin

RESOURCES

UNITED STATES

National Domestic Violence Hotline - Website: thehotline.org, Telephone: 1-800-799-SAFE (7233).

One Love - Website: joinonelove.org

CANADA

Assaulted Women's Helpline (Canada) - Website: https://www.awhl.org/, Telephone: 1-866-863-0511

UNITED KINGDOM

National Domestic Abuse Helpline (U.K.) - Website: https://www.nationaldahelpline.org.uk/, Telephone: 0808 2000 247

AUSTRALIA

National Domestic Family and Sexual Violence Counselling Service - Website: https://www.1800respect.org.au/, Telephone: 1-800-RESPECT (737-732)

REFERENCES

Ackerman, C. (2018, November 6). *What is Self-Worth & How Do We Build it? (Incl. Worksheets).* Positive Psychology. https://positivepsychology.com/self-worth/

Adams, S. (2022, January 17). *How to Find Peace After a Toxic Relationship.* Develop Good Habits. https://www.developgoodhabits.com/peace-toxic-relationship/

Alexander, M. (2020, September 23). *7 Keys to Effective Communication Skills in Relationships.* Seattle Christian Counseling. https://seattlechristiancounseling.com/articles/7-keys-to-effective-communication-skills-in-relationships

Batoon, A. (2021, November 1). *13 Tips for How to Heal from a Toxic Relationship.* Modern Intimacy. https://www.modernintimacy.com/13-tips-for-how-to-heal-from-a-toxic-relationship/

Borchardt, L. (n.d.) *30% of Women in the GGS Community Have Likely Experienced Domestic Abuse.* https://www.girlsgonestrong.com/blog/articles/domestic-abuse/

Braithwaite, P. (2021, March 16). *10 Ways to Let Go of Anger (Without Ignoring It).* Self. https://www.self.com/story/how-to-let-go-of-anger

Brickel, R. (2024). *Healthy Relationships Matter More Than We Think.* PsychAlive. https://www.psychalive.org/healthy-relationships-matter/

Brister, N. (2021, May 19). *Why Forgiveness Is So Hard but Important.* Psychology Today. https://www.psychologytoday.com/ca/blog/your-emotional-meter/202105/why-forgiveness-is-so-hard-important

Caraballo, J. (2018, July 9). *Is it Possible (or Necessary) to Get Relationship Closure?.* Talkspace. https://www.talkspace.com/blog/relationship-closure-possible-necessary/

Cicurel, D. (2024, March). *Toxic relationships: 8 ways to move on after a break up.* Stylist. https://www.stylist.co.uk/life/how-to-move-on-from-a-toxic-relationship-to-become-a-stronger-person-argument-couples-sex-sadness-man-woman/65317

Craft, A. (2022, February 10). *Signs of Mental Abuse*. Healthline. https://www.healthline.com/health/signs-of-mental-abuse

Cuncic, A. (2021, October 18). *3 Steps to Better Communication*. ReachOut. https://au.reachout.com/articles/3-steps-to-better-communication

Daskal, L. (2019, July 31). *35 Signs You're in a Toxic Business Relationship*. Inc. https://www.inc.com/lolly-daskal/35-signs-youre-in-a-toxic-business-relationship.html

Davis, T. (2023, December 12). *6 Ways to Build Self-Esteem*. Psychology Today. https://www.psychologytoday.com/ca/blog/click-here-happiness/202202/6-ways-build-self-esteem

Enright, R., North, J. (1998). *Exploring Forgiveness*. https://trans4mind.com/counterpoint/life-challenges/life-challenges-pdfs/Exploring_Forgiveness.pdf

Family Centre. (2019, December 31). *5 Tips for Setting Boundaries in Relationships*. https://www.familycentre.org/news/post/5-tips-for-setting-boundaries-in-relationships

Firestone, L. (2022, June 6). *How to Recover from a Toxic Relationship*. Psychology Today. https://www.psychologytoday.com/ca/blog/here-there-and-everywhere/202206/how-recover-toxic-relationship

Fitzgibbons. (1998). "Anger and the Healing Power of Forgiveness" in *Exploring Forgiveness*. https://trans4mind.com/counterpoint/life-challenges/life-challenges-pdfs/Exploring_Forgiveness.pdf

Forbes. (2022, January 5). *10 Daily Habits of the Most Confident People*. https://www.inc.com/chris-dessi/10-daily-habits-of-the-most-confident-people.html

Gillis, K. (2022, July 1). *6 Steps Toward Recovery From a Toxic Relationship*. Psychology Today. https://www.psychologytoday.com/ca/blog/invisible-bruises/202207/6-steps-toward-recovery-toxic-relationship

Gottman, J; Silver, N. (1999). *The Seven Principles for Making Marriage Work*. Crown Publishers imprint (Three Rivers Press).

Gourani, S. (2019, November 24). *What Does Having a Real Family Mean?* Forbes. https://www.forbes.com/sites/soulaimagourani/2019/11/24/what-does-having-a-real-family-mean/

Graebner, K. (2021, June 18). *How to practice self compassion and tame your inner critic*. BetterUp. https://www.betterup.com/blog/self-compassion

Hall, J., Freedman, S., & Hegarty, K. (2019). *A Review of the Empirical Research Using Enright's Process Model of Interpersonal Forgiveness.*

ResearchGate. https://www.researchgate.net/publication/337445184_A_Review_of_the_Empirical_Research_Using_Enright's_Process_Model_of_Interpersonal_Forgiveness

Haran, M. (2020, November 5). *Anxiety and Anger*. Discovery Mood. https://discoverymood.com/blog/anxiety-and-anger/

Huie, J. L. (n.d.). *Quotes about New Beginnings*. https://www.jonathanlockwoodhuie.com/quotes/new_beginnings

Jed Foundation. (n.d.). *How to Safely End Unhealthy Relationships*. https://jedfoundation.org/resource/how-to-safely-end-unhealthy-relationships/

Karney, C. (2022, July 5). *6 Steps Toward Recovery from a Toxic Relationship*. Psychology Today. https://www.psychologytoday.com/ca/blog/invisible-bruises/202207/6-steps-toward-recovery-toxic-relationship

Lancer, D. (2016, May 31). *Relationship Closure: Is It Possible and Necessary?* Talkspace. https://www.talkspace.com/blog/relationship-closure-possible-necessary/

Lebow, H. (2021, June 10). *How Childhood Trauma May Affect Adult Relationships*. PsychCentral. https://psychcentral.com/blog/how-childhood-trauma-affects-adult-relationships

Lichtenfield, S., Buechner, V., Maier, M., and Fernandez-Capo, M. (2015, May 6). *Forgive and Forget: Differences between Decisional and Emotional Forgiveness*. National Library of Medicine. https://www.ncbi.nlm.nih.gov/pmc/articles/PMC4422736/

Love is respect. (n.d.). *Relationship spectrum*. https://www.loveisrespect.org/everyone-deserves-a-healthy-relationship/relationship-spectrum/

Mantra Care. (n.d.). *Toxic Relationship Counseling*. https://mantracare.org/therapy/relationship/toxic-relationship-counseling/

Mapes, D. (2011, August 22). *Toxic Friends: 8 in 10 People Endure Poisonous Pals*. Today. https://www.today.com/health/toxic-friends-8-10-people-endure-poisonous-pals-1C9413205

Marriage.com. (n.d.). *How to Recover from a Toxic Relationship*. https://www.marriage.com/advice/relationship/how-to-recover-from-a-toxic-relationship/

Mayo Clinic. (n.d.). *Forgiveness: Letting Go of Grudges and Bitterness*. https://www.mayoclinic.org/healthy-lifestyle/adult-health/in-depth/forgiveness/art-20047692

McGill University Counselling Service. (n.d.). *Helpful Hints for Building*

Self-Esteem. https://www.mcgill.ca/counselling/files/counselling/self-esteem_helpful_hints_0.pdf

McQueen, J. (2021, April 9). *How to Handle Toxic Family Members.* WebMD. https://www.webmd.com/mental-health/features/handle-toxic-family

Mead, D. (2016, April 8). *What Causes Codependency?* Psych Central. https://psychcentral.com/blog/imperfect/2016/04/what-causes-codependency

Moore, C. (2019, June 2). *How to Practice Self-Compassion: 8 Techniques and Tips.* Positive Psychology. https://positivepsychology.com/how-to-practice-self-compassion/

National Coalition Against Domestic Violence. (n.d.). *Statistics.* NCADV. https://ncadv.org/STATISTICS

National Domestic Violence Hotline. (n.d.). *Is This Abuse?* https://www.thehotline.org/is-this-abuse/

Neuharth, D. (2018, November 8). *How to Deal with a Narcissist: Narcissistic Relationship.* GoodTherapy. https://www.goodtherapy.org/learn-about-therapy/issues/narcissism/how-to-deal

New York State. (n.d.). *What Does a Healthy Relationship Look Like?* https://www.ny.gov/teen-dating-violence-awareness-and-prevention/what-does-healthy-relationship-look

Neumann, I., Veenema, A., Beiderbeck, D. (2010, March 30). *Aggression and Anxiety: Social Context and Neurobiological Links.* https://www.ncbi.nlm.nih.gov/pmc/articles/PMC2854527

Noreen, S., and MacLeod, M. (2021). *Moving on or deciding to let go? A pathway exploring the relationship between emotional and decisional forgiveness and intentional forgetting.* American Psychology Association. https://psycnet.apa.org/record/2020-64856-001

One Love Foundation. (2020, November 13). *7 Tips for Handling Conflict in Your Relationship.* https://www.joinonelove.org/learn/handling_conflict/

One Love Foundation. (n.d.). *5 Places for Help You May Not Have Known.* https://www.joinonelove.org/learn/5-places-for-help-may-not-known/

Pattemore, C. (2021, June 3). *10 Ways to Build and Preserve Better Boundaries.* PsychCentral. https://psychcentral.com/lib/10-way-to-build-and-preserve-better-boundaries

Peace Over Violence. (n.d.). *The Cycle of Violence and Power and Control.*

https://www.peaceoverviolence.org/iii-the-cycle-of-violence-and-power-and-control

Raypole, C. (2020, November 30). *Understanding the Cycle of Abuse*. https://www.healthline.com/health/relationships/cycle-of-abuse#the-cycle

ReachOut. (n.d.). *3 Steps to Better Communication*. https://au.reachout.com/articles/3-steps-to-better-communication

Relationship Institute. (1999). *The Seven Principles for Making Marriage Work (Summary)*. https://relationshipinstitute.com.au/uploads/resources/the_seven_principles_for_making_marriage_work_summary.pdf

Ripes, J. (2021, April 21). *13 Tips for How to Heal from a Toxic Relationship*. Modern Intimacy. https://www.modernintimacy.com/13-tips-for-how-to-heal-from-a-toxic-relationship/

Scott, E. (2023, November 3). *What to Know If You're Concerned About a Toxic Relationship*. https://www.verywellmind.com/toxic-relationships-4174665

Selva, J. (2018, February 9). *Codependency: What Are The Signs & How To Overcome It*. Positive Psychology. https://positivepsychology.com/codependency-definition-signs-worksheets/

Smith, K. (2022, April 5). *Why You Should Forgive But 'Never' Forget*. PsychCentral. https://psychcentral.com/health/reasons-to-forgive-but-not-forget

Smith, M., Segal, J. (n.d.) *Domestic Violence and Abuse*. HelpGuide. https://www.helpguide.org/articles/abuse/domestic-violence-and-abuse.htm

Scott, E. (2023, November 3). *What to Know If You're Concerned About a Toxic Relationship: How to Spot the Signs of a Toxic Relationship*. Verywell Mind. https://www.verywellmind.com/toxic-relationships-4174665

Stevens, J. (2012, October 3). *The Adverse Childhood Experiences Study*. ACESTooHigh LLC. https://acestoohigh.com/2012/10/03/the-adverse-childhood-experiences-study-the-largest-most-important-public-health-study-you-never-heard-of-began-in-an-obesity-clinic/

The Forgiveness Project. (n.d.). *Stories*. https://www.theforgivenessproject.com/stories/

The Forgiveness Project. (n.d.). *The Forgiveness Toolbox*. https://www.theforgivenessproject.com/resources/forgiveness-tool-boxes/

Van Edwards, V. (2024, June 4). *6 Effective Tips to Politely Say No (that actually work!)*. https://www.scienceofpeople.com/how-to-say-no/

Vincenty, S. (2022). *How to Find Inner Peace in the Chaos*. Oprah Daily. https://www.oprahdaily.com/life/a29474453/how-to-find-inner-peace/

www.ingramcontent.com/pod-product-compliance
Lightning Source LLC
Chambersburg PA
CBHW072200070526
44585CB00015B/1226